WHY

LESSONS IN GOD'S THEME PARK,

IN THE POWER OF HIS RESURRECTION

RUSSELL DAVID HOBBS

WHY, Lessons in God's Theme Park, In the Power of His Resurrection: Trilogy Christian Publishers A Wholly Owned Subsidiary of Trinity Broadcasting Network

2442 Michelle Drive Tustin, CA 92780

Manufactured in the United States of America

10 9 8 7 6 5 4 3 2 1

Library of Congress Cataloging-in-Publication Data is available.

ISBN: 978-1-63769-336-0

E-ISBN: 978-1-63769-337-7

DEDICATION

This book is dedicated to my mom for encouraging me all of my life and her patience with me through the process, and to my dad for teaching me to love truth even when it is uncomfortable.

AUTHOR'S NOTE

This book is not long; I encourage you to take time to prayerfully read the scripture references as you read through and let God give you additional revelation.

TABLE OF CONTENTS

PREFACE

Most books are forwarded by men who appreciate and are friends of the writer. This book is forwarded by God's prophetic Word for the writer. This is the greatest endorsement one can have.

The Word of the Lord 4/21/95 as given to the writer by Prophet David Fees of the Early Church in Plano, Texas.

"I see you like Josiah: he read the Word, and when he discovered what was in the Word, it shocked him, and he went whole-hearted toward the goal God had given him; he was radical. The other kings did things to a measure, but Josiah cleaned house. When he saw that you were supposed to celebrate the Passover, he did the Passover; when he saw that you were supposed to clean out the temple, he cleaned out the temple, he had all the garbage cleaned out, he would not let up. I see you have the spirit of Josiah upon you; you have been ridiculed and mocked for that; that's okay. Every person who is an extremist makes enemies; you're an extremist, you can't do things partway. God made you that way when you see something wrong and something that has to be done. God commands you, you just go and do it and do it with zeal and abandon, you don't care what people think, you do it to the nth degree. God has put that spirit in you; don't apologize for it, God has made you that way, and you'll

make enemies, but you'll get things done that nobody else can get done, you see; allow God to perfect you in that. I see you being raised up in the House of the Lord for a mighty work, and the day is going to come when God is going to use you to clean house. I see you cleaning up an area; you're a radical, you're called to be a radical, not halfway; don't play it safe, you're a pioneer, you'll be on the front line."

WHY?

Why did God create this whole universe as He did with physical planets, stars, animals, and people?

He could have made it differently. He could have made it all spiritual, everything floating around in an ooey-gooey mess of lovey-dovey stuff. He could have made it with four-headed creatures spawning little creatures. When we realize the plants, the trees, reproduction, even the weather, the rain, and the harvest are all pictures of His ways and prove His existence, we then have a valuable key to interpret the creation (Romans 1:18-21).

God created this whole creation to show His love to His created ones, display His glory and teach a great moral to this story; a created thing cannot survive without its creator! Love cannot be known unless it is received.

The fall of man was all an issue of independence; love is displayed in the great reunion. The sacrificial love displayed at Calvary is the reason for this creation, a drama created by the great artist to communicate to us the ultimate love.

The entire Bible is tied together by one central theme, that of death, burial, and resurrection, or we could call it sacrifice, waiting, and new life.

The whole creation is "God's theme park," the theme is death, burial, and resurrection. Which came first, the pattern of creation or the coming of Christ? The pattern of creation is seen in fruit that falls to the ground, is buried, and then rises in a new plant or the caterpillar enters the cocoon tomb and then emerges as a butterfly. Did this start only after Jesus Christ rose from the dead? No, He was manifest in the fullness of time to confirm all that creation had been screaming for thousands of years. The laws of death, burial, and resurrection (the gospel) were set in motion from the time of creation. This was God's design to reveal His purpose through all time to His saints. Romans 1:20 says that the invisible things can be understood by the things that are seen. The point here, however, is that many Christian's beliefs contradict the creation! All flesh wants the resurrection of life, but not everyone wants to die and be buried. The new age-humanists love to steal principles from Jesus' teaching, they talk about love, abundant life, and resurrection, but these are impossible without sacrifice, paying the price, and death to the carnal man! We are either in Christ or we are Antichrist; no one is neutral.

MAN'S CHANCE

Israel could not keep a covenant with God, and no one else can either. God had to come and do it Himself in Jesus Christ. Many preachers talk of God's remnant in Israel, "the faithful few," but even these all failed in the flesh to keep the covenant. Abraham compromised, David murdered, and even Rahab, the harlot, was justified by lying. We must conclude that no one lived a perfect life, nor did God expect they would. These people are all in the "Hall of Faith" (Hebrews 11). The Old Testament saints were saved by grace through faith, just as we are today. In Hebrews 8-10, we see that the priesthood of Moses was not perfect, weak in flesh; it was only a shadow of the resurrected priesthood. Jesus, the author and finisher of our faith, was born in the flesh in obscurity, was obedient all the way through a normal servant's life, then perfect in public ministry, and finally accomplished the real purpose of His life, being offered as "the lamb." He was able to enter into the heavens and establish the eternal priesthood, the perfect covenant, with no chance of failure because it doesn't depend on us. As David said, "Oh Lord, my hope is in your mercy." The Creator and creation became one in the Messiah. It would have been impossible to have a Christ or Messiah without the creation. We, the Church, keep a covenant with God only because we are "dead and hid in Christ." He does it through us because we cannot!

(Colossians 3) All glory must be given to God; no flesh will glory in His presence. No man has ever lived a perfect life; no man will ever live a perfect life. Only God can do it. He slays us and lives through us to accomplish His eternal desire and to spoil Lucifer by proving that to serve is love! (Isaiah 14:12-15) Our nature is to seek the best place for ourselves; God's nature is to sacrifice comfort, reputation, control to make others happy.

Jesus Christ, the second Adam, took on the creation, clothed in humanity. He took the creation through death, burial, and resurrection so that we may experience eternal glory. Jesus brought heaven to earth, and He took earth up to heaven; this was His plan all along (Ephesians 1:9-10). He did not ask us if he could. Without revelation, we didn't even know a need to be redeemed, much less desire to go through the process. The flesh cannot enter into the "Promised Land." Moses is a picture of Christ, but Joshua is a better picture of Christ. Moses could not enter in the promised land, he failed, weakened by his humanity, vexed by the people, the demands, lack of vision, he had to stay back, but Joshua—the same name as Jesus Yeshua, "deliverer,"— took the people into the promised land.In another picture, we see Aaron, the priest, born of man and woman; he was good on his good days, but not good enough. Melchizedek was a perfect priest; why, because he was not tied to sinful flesh. Melchizedek was without origin, like the ultimate high priest Jesus Christ. Born of the virgin, not hindered by the curses through the fallen blood line, Jesus was able to keep a covenant with God perfectly (Hebrews 7). God must come into a vessel to impart power sufficient to reign over Satan. Lucifer is supernatural, and only by the power of the Anointed One living in us can we now rule and reign over darkness. Since the day of God's visitation in Israel, the story is the same; people who think they can do it (keep the law) miss the promise of God's spirit. The blessings of Abraham can only be received by those who admit they are not righteous; this death to self-positions us to be born as Sons of God. Our inheritance as Abraham's seed in Christ is filled with blessings, but as long as we strive to make it on our own, we frustrate the grace of God (Galatians 2:20-21).

WHAT IS GOD UP TO?

To understand God's purpose in this creation, one must understand the resurrection. To understand resurrection, one must understand death to self. The Bible is understood only when interpreted by the Holy Spirit through the revelation of resurrection. Life, with all its pain and suffering, seems useless without this revelation. Through the toil of eating, drinking, career, and work, man searches for his purpose; this temporal existence is only the medium in which God, the great artist, performs His eternal sculpture in our hearts. We get so unraveled by trials, pain, and loss, but these are designed that we may know Him, like the happy child in the wheelchair; our hearts are free of temporal perspective. David said, "Lord, why do the wicked prosper and have many children, but the righteous are afflicted?" When God is dealing with a person to form Christ in them, their life may not look so good from the outside, while others seem so successful because God has not called them. The most significant event in pre-Adamic time was the fall of Lucifer. Lucifer, being lifted up in His heart, rebelled and was cast down. To prove to the angelic host, the Glory of God, the Almighty created man in His own image to surpass the created Lucifer. Job knew the revelation of resurrection, which allowed him to stay faithful to God (Job1:8). To prove that only God can be God, man was created higher than angels in the image of God. In Hebrews 1and Psalm 8, we see where man is referred to as "lower than the angels, but before the fall, man was higher than the angels." Adam, with free will, "chose to be like God" and fell, then God Himself had to become the second Adam to prove the dependency of all created beings (Genesis 3:5, Romans 8:29).

Today religious ones are still trying to be "like God" without death, burial, and resurrection. Believe it or not, this is Antichrist (instead of Christ). It is a self-righteous posture to think that one could ever be like Jesus the Christ; Christ in you is the hope of glory and the hope of ever walking in love.

Abraham is the ultimate picture of dependency on God. He was counted righteous by "believing" but still tried flesh works to help God. Only after God allowed him to try to fulfill the promise and fail (Ishmael) did God fulfill the promise. This was God's plan all along. Resurrection is God's prime mode of operation in displaying His glory. First, He made angels able to fall, able to desire being worshipped, but not in his likeness. Then he made man able to fall, able to desire worship, and in His likeness, man is unlimited in creative power: like God, we can imagine and then create. Still, man is not God. This is the theme of creation. Man needs God before the fall, during the redemption period, and throughout eternity. Nowhere in the Bible is seen a true overcomer except the incarnate Christ. He knew the revelation of death, burial, and resurrection. Faith works by love! (Galatians 5:6) Jesus' loyalty to truth, the love for us, and His Father allowed Him to accomplish redemption. God wants to work the same process of death, burial, and resurrection through our lives to reach multitudes. Abraham saw this revelation before he offered His son up for sacrifice. "If He dies God can raise Him from the dead; God gave Him, He can re-give Him"(see Hebrews 11:19, paraphrased here). This exceeds "God providing," but this is elementary school faith; he wants to take us deeper into "of course He provides, what is He really up to?"

God could only request Abraham to offer his son because He was to offer His on in the fullness of time (Isaiah 53:10).

HAVE YOU SEEN YOUR DEATH YET?

Joseph saw his time of death when he was being betrayed. The dungeon was his time of burial to bring forth his resurrection. Moses died to the pleasures of Egypt, and then the wilderness for forty years was his burial. Finally, God resurrected him and took him back to Egypt, ready for ministry. The best picture of death, of course, is Gethsemane, where even the Lord prayed, "Not my will, but yours be done," sweating drops of blood as the cup was given Him, all the sin of the world, sorrow, rejection, abandonment, all that Adam had sown and we have all reaped, came on Christ in this death.

Your death may be working as a janitor while liberating sermons boil in your heart; it may be giving up a relationship that "feels" so right, but you know God has other plans, it may be keeping your mouth shut while your boss steals all your ideas and receives acclaim and riches. God designs each saint's life to be one death after another because this is where we come to "know" Him (Philippians 3:10).

In New Testament scripture, we are given revelation to God's ways—we don't have to fast or pray or work for these pieces of liberating truth. In 1 Corinthians 1:26-29, we see

21

the point of the resurrection driven home again. Not many
wise, not many strong, not many noble are called or used by
God, so then no flesh shall glory in His presence. In children's Bibles, the pictures of Samson always show a great
big handsome muscle man. I'll bet you a thousand hallelu-
jahs that Samson looked more like Barney Fife. Gideon was
hiding at the threshing floor when God called the "mighty
man of valor." Moses was a man with a speech problem, yet
God called him to speak to Pharaoh. To kill all hope of self;
as Paul puts it in (Philippians 3:3-6), "all confidence in the
flesh," God called "unlearned men," tax collectors and fish-
ermen to be the Apostles of the church, to reach the world
with the gospel. This is the way of God. He will bring affliction to a person to kill all self-confidence (whether physical,
financial, or mental), then we are humbled to receive "the
mind of Christ," then He gives faith for deliverance. He will
then deliver us into the resurrection life; as a new creature
with a testimony, we give Him all the glory! (Psalm 119:75-
76) It is popular in these apostate times to say that God does
not afflict anyone, but Psalm 119:75 proves that God is faithful to afflict us to accomplish His eternal purpose that none
of us would volunteer for. Let's consider a real-life example. A sister gets a prophetic word in church; "You will be a
great Psalmist for the Lord; many will be delivered by your
anointed songs." This sister had been a famous singer before
she was saved, and now many expectations were on her to be
"great for God." Well, after years go by, and she is learning

discipleship and the kingdom of God, she develops a growth in her throat, doctors can do nothing, she goes through all the rituals of being prayed for, confessing her healing, etc. All the people at church rebuke the devil because "God doesn't hurt anyone," but she still can't sing. The people in the church, like "Job's friends," may come around telling her there must be sin in her life or she doesn't have enough faith. Sometimes we judge matters in our limited perspective and try to figure things out, causing people even more sorrow. She finally gives up, just like Abraham did when he lay with his maid and had Ishmael, or as he did after the "son of the flesh" had grown up, and it was obvious he was not what God had promised. Now, this sweet sister is free to be a person in the body with no special expectations on her. She begins to enjoy the little things in life, like children and flowers; people are even delivered to her church without her singing. She has work done in her heart; now, she loves God for who He is, not what He is going to do for her. Then in the fullness of God's time, one day, some nobody in the church prays for her, and she is instantly healed. She begins to sing and prophesy of the goodness of the Lord, spontaneous combustion praise breaks forth in the church, and her prophecy is fulfilled! The key here is that the prophecy is fulfilled by God, not by voice lessons, doctors, or leadership trying to help God do His job. The Lord's main work of art is in the hearts of His people, He wants us to know love, sacrifice, to prefer each other above ourselves, and He will do whatever it takes to accomplish this. Many would argue whether God or the devil put the sickness, the growth on her throat; in 1 Kings 22:20-23, we see that the Lord used a lying Spirit for His purpose, in Isaiah 54:16, God says he created the waster to destroy, and in 2 Kings 15:5, God smote an idolatrous king with leprosy, he was never healed. We know God does love His people, but our understanding of His long-term ways is limited. He chastens those He loves, and His tools for chastening are trials, tribulations, and the devil. The body of Christ has two main extremes; on the "faith" side, we see a bunch of selfish brats "claiming" all the toys they want for "their little kingdom," stepping on each other to get to "the man of God" who will touch them and all their dreams will come true. Then on the other side, we have the false humility, religious ones who think the sicker and poor we are, the more spiritual we are. Both of these perversions are wrong. Yes, the Lord will prosper us, but a fool with a lot of money is a blemish on the Body of Christ (James 4:1-5). The death, burial, and resurrection pictured throughout the Bible is God's agenda! We have our agendas; many saints are hoping and praying for this or that, but the prayers that are always answered are the prayers according to God's will, the prayers for wisdom, revelation, and to be conformed to the image of Christ. The desire of the Father is to give us the kingdom, but first, He must make us able to rule in love. God's agenda is to bring us to death so Christ can live and love through us, then we are "anointed," broken vessels he can pour through. Paul said, "I die daily." If this is a reality in your life, you can also say, "I'm resurrected daily!"

THE APPLE

Once a person receives the revelation of resurrection, it is impossible to read the Bible without seeing it on every page. The amazing thing is that God can be known through this revelation just by looking at the creation and quickened by the Holy Spirit. Throughout history, most of God's remnant have not owned Bibles. Taught by the Spirit and creation, Abraham, Moses, and Job all received the revelation of resurrection. Today millions of people have the whole Bible and know nothing. When we look at an apple tree, we see seeds fall to the ground (death), it stays in the dirt (burial), and then sprouts (resurrection), but it doesn't stop there. The new sprout grows up and bears more fruit which falls to the ground and brings more trees than before. The apple is like our body; the seed inside is the Word of God (1 Peter 1:23). Our outward man perishes (the meat of the apple rots), but the inward man is renewed day by day; the word grows in us (Christ is formed in us) and lives on eternal. The Christ in us is sown into the lives around us and brings forth fruit; whether it be our congregation, family, friends, or even our enemies, God wants people to feed off of us. The fruit of the Spirit draws people to us to receive the Word and the kingdom.

The first Israel was Jacob (the man), out of his loins came the second Israel (the nation), and out of the nation came the last Israel (the church), the "Holy Nation" (1 Peter 2:9). Jacob was a good example of resurrection. The deceiver had schemed all his life to get his way; God broke him and made him the Father of many nations. Romans 9 shows that "because of the purpose of election," the older (Esau) shall serve the younger (Jacob). This is God's way to get it through our thick skulls. Saul was better equipped to slay Goliath than David, but David was anointed, and that is the difference. Anointed means "God is with you"—it's that simple. Back to the apple, the physical creation is a manifestation of the great parables of God's heart. Old covenant Israel is the forerunner of the Church, both Jews and Gentiles, God's chosen people. In Israel's failure to enter into the rest (Hebrews 3:10), we see that unbelief or self-confidence is the enemy of God, but in Hebrews 4:3, we see that belief is all it takes to enter. Now the real question is, "Believe what?" Everybody "believes" Jesus was the Son of God, etc., but Abraham was made (after much affliction) to believe that God not only could deliver on His promise but even raise Isaac from the dead if need be. The difference between Caleb and the other spies was that Caleb knew that these giants were grasshoppers to God. The difference between David and Saul was, David knew God, and nothing is too difficult for the Lord.The difference between David and Goliath was David put his trust in God, and Goliath trusted his own power (and so do the uncircumcised until this day); this is the spirit of Antichrist. The Antichrist is not seen in rock bands that say "hail Satan," these guys are deceived and rebelling against religion. The Antichrist is seen in self-righteous "religious" ones who oppose the work of the Holy Spirit and trust in their own power to "serve God." Saul was killing Christians until he met Jesus in Spirit, many seminaries pump out Saul's today who work against the Holy Spirit by denouncing the current move of the Spirit. Like Stephen said, "How long will you resist the Holy Spirit?" The problem comes when we think that God will deliver us the way we think he should deliver. We all know David is a picture of Christ, but God did not deliver Christ from the Romans and the envious religious Jews. He has a greater deliverance in mind; death, burial, and resurrection! Only through the process of death, burial, and resurrection can there be a new creation (2 Corinthians 5:17). We must stop trying to save ourselves so that God can use us. Jesus is the first born among many brethren (Romans 8:29). The first creation died with Adam, then was cursed, but the second Adam came and has been sown into the first creation and has raised it into incorruption (1 Corinthians 15:42-44), the first creation being an apple of sorts, as, in Revelation 14:4, Moses led the Jews out of Egypt and to the wilderness, but Joshua had to take them over into the Promised Land—something that the flesh could not do because it was weak. The Spirit had to do it (Romans 8:2-4). Many Christians lead "holy" lives in the flesh, having a form of godliness but deny the power thereof, but they cannot enter the Promised Land life without the fullness of the Spirit. The fruit and the gifts are evident in resurrection people. The Holy Spirit led Israel to the wilderness to be tempted and tested, weak in the flesh, and they fell in unbelief and self-confidence. This was to show us that "we" cannot do it; the flesh cannot walk with God and accomplish His work. The Holy Spirit led Jesus to the wilderness to be tempted and tested like Israel, with humanity on His shoulders, He overcame by faith in the Word, but the difference is that Jesus walked in perfect love; He cared not for Himself. Therefore, Satan could find nothing in Him, no place to snare Him. When we are willing to die for our brethren, we will not sin, and the law is fulfilled in love. The disciples all lived with Jesus and even did miracles, but they denied Him and could not "see" the revelation of the kingdom until they had failed, and later in the upper room, they all received the promise of the Father, the Holy Spirit. Now with Christ in them, they could see and overcome. Again, the flesh (man) was not able to receive the things of God, for they are spiritually discerned; only the regenerated Spirit of man can "see" the kingdom (John 3:3).

HAVE YOU EVER DONE NOTHING?

God enjoys taking an "impossible" situation and confounding the wise and prudent by bringing life from death. Abraham and Sarah were too old in the natural to have a child, no sperm, no eggs. A perfect couple for God to work with, even these two famous "Hall of Faith" saints tried to help God out. We all know the story well, but how does it apply to our lives? Okay, have you ever done nothing? We all have dreams, visions, and promises from God. Until we know that we are "in the faith," God can't use us. Paul said,"Test yourself to see if you are in the faith." On the basic questions of salvation, have you ever done nothing? As in exhausted to the point that you did not pray, did not read your Bible, did not go to church,and did not try to control your mind to believe in Jesus? When you stopped holding on with all your being to believe, what happened? Did the earth stop rotating, did the sky fall, and did your face fall off, anything? Did you hear God talk to you? Were you still saved? You say, "God forbid, I would never do that!" Well, until a believer has done nothing and then discovered that Christ is really in them, they are still an actor. If we are not able to believe that God is able to keep us without our help, how can we believe He can use us to save others or work miracles?

The only true motive to do the works of God is out of love for Him. We read the Bible to get to know Him; we go to church to praise Him and serve the saints and learn of Him. We must come to death and burial and then see that He has "raised us into a newness of life" (Ephesians 2:5-6). Most believers are afraid to question the faith or ask God things they are really feeling. The more honest we are with someone, the deeper the relationship can grow. Intimacy comes from vulnerability. How much more can we trust the Lord? He died for us when we were still sinners. How much more is He for us now? He knows all your thoughts anyway, but you might as well tell Him how you feel. God is not fragile; neither is our salvation and relationship with Him. He came to save us; He created the creation with redemption as part of the plan; no one can snatch us out of His hand; come on, *get real!* (John 10:28-30) It is the same with our ministry or dreams; we must wait for God to open doors, we must become content with the little things, with our relationship with Jesus, like David in the obscure wilderness tending the sheep, praising God, and God knows where to find you. If and when God wants to exalt you, He will, and then you will be a true representative of Jesus.

Once we are dead and hidden in Christ, *His* voice is inside of us quick like lightning, speaking to us anytime we listen, sometimes even when we are not. The Word of God is quick and powerful, sharper than any two-edged sword

(Hebrews 4:12).This is referring to the Rhema Word, not the logos written word.We must believe He is in us and loves us faithfully every second of every day, and then realizing He is speaking becomes easier. God speaks to all people, not only His that are already regenerated, but He speaks to everyone. God the Word is holding the world together by the power of His word. He whispers to the atheist,"Go home,'"'Go see your friend," or "Go to bed early"; as the shepherd, He directs all the people constantly orchestrating the affairs of man to fulfill His plans. Yes, He watches over, protects, directs, and guides even the ones who deny His existence.We, who are are already adopted into His eternal family of love, certainly know His faithfulness; that still small voice is proven over time. We can all look back at many times He was talking to us, but perhaps we didn't listen, the Holy Spirit's whisper is always there, we all know it's true, He is in us,He's with us, and He's keeping us every day by His power. "Who are kept by the power of God through faith for salvation ready to be revealed in the last time"(1 Peter 1:5).

31

THE COMFORT ZONE

The disciples did not yet understand the revelation of resurrection, so Jesus told them clearly to their faces, "I must be rejected of men and die." They could not fathom; they wanted to physically reign in the old city of Jerusalem right then. Our carnal mind wants to use Jesus and faith to build our lives, our kingdom, our church, but God is love, and His purpose is eternal. Many Christians today want Jesus to give them all these gifts and prosperity, but He is working on a much more important and eternal project. We want the presents under the "Christmas tree," but He wants to give us His presence under the "tree of Calvary." We must approach Jesus and say, "Slay me, Lord, that I may know you in the fellowship of your sufferings and in the power of your resurrection" (Philippians 3:10-11). When we are made conformable to His death, we can know His love, His presence, the joy unspeakable and full of glory. It is conformable, not comfortable! Nothing good ever comes from being comfortable. The flesh will never volunteer to enter into suffering; it is by the Holy Spirit that God accomplishes this.

In America, we all have cars, houses, and internet, mobile devices; how can we know suffering? In each era, God has designed men's lives to be a training ground for His process of conforming us. In this highly technological age of comfort, we may not wake with the rooster to work the field for food, but we do know stress, anxiety, and other emotional and mental testing. To know Him in the power of His resurrection, we must also know Him in His sufferings. To accomplish this, we must be made conformable to His death (Philippians 3:10). This is a work of the Spirit; some will read this and exactly know what we are talking about, while others will learn this over the seasons ahead. The Lord sees to it that all saints who have fully surrendered hear of His surgery and then experience it. We all want to get what we want, to live a fully meaningful life with comfort and security, but we get to know Christ in trials, hardship, disappointment, and loneliness. These are all ingredients of "the fellowship of His suffering," how we "get to know" Him. In the trials, we learn to say "thank you, Lord" and really mean it, but the thing we are thanking Him, for now, is that our names are written in the Lamb's Book of Life, for His steadfast friendship and that He does provide food, shelter, and clothing. The path that Jesus Christ walked is our path too. He lives through us here and now, letting us be rejected, misunderstood, lonely, and even slain to show His unconditional love to the world, at the same time, making us His faithful Bride. Love your enemy, go the extra mile, pray for those who use you, if they want your coat, give your shirt as well. This love cannot be imitated; this love is found only in Christ and in His dear ones (see the Course of the Word later in this book).

The flesh will not "enter in" voluntarily. No amount of altar calls on Sunday will produce a "Christian," it is the real life during the week when Christ does the deep work on us. People can pray, fast, read the Bible, sing songs and preach all kinds of religious acts in the flesh. Religions all over the world practice all these without the Holy Spirit, even with unclean Spirits (Matthew 7:21-23). It is on the job we don't like with people we don't like, in a world we don't like, that we get to know Jesus and learn of His suffering. This momentary light affliction will produce a far more exceeding weight of glory. God's agenda is long-term; He is faithful even when we are not, to produce in and through us a work that all will be proud of for eternity. The wilderness or dungeon is God's design to bring us to His jealous love. Joseph said, "What you meant for evil, God meant for good" (Genesis 50:20). Most people today say that God "allowed" Joseph's brothers to treat their little brother cruelly, and then God turned the situation around for good. The Word of God says over and over that in His sovereignty, the Lord orchestrates these things to display His glory (Proverbs 21:1, Revelation 17:17). The Hebrew word for "meant" in Genesis 50:20 is Chashab, "to fabricate," "to plot," this proves that God is in control; He is not following the devil around fixing things. God gave Joseph His dream, knowing he would tell his brothers,God wanted Joseph to be a slave; He orchestrated this whole scenario to setup Israel's bondage, deliverance, and destiny, to show us His ways. When

35

a man has the opportunity to save someone's life and does not try, even an earthly court rules "negligence."God is the initiator, not Satan.

Many "faith" preachers cannot deal with this because it renders their "formulas" ineffective. Like the person who says a car wreck scared them back to the Lord, then everybody blames the devil for the car wreck, well that makes Satan the best evangelist in the world, which is preposterous! Many car wrecks may just be a human error; neither God nor the devil caused them. The devil is blamed, or I should say, gets credit for much more than he actually does or has the power to do. He lies and causes man to destroy himself many times. Today Christians sin and blame the devil, just like Eve did. Joseph was taken to Egypt as a slave to redeem later the elect, a picture of Christ that was God's plan for Joseph. God doesn't wait for the devil to do something, then "use it for good." God's ways are above our ways, His thoughts higher than our thoughts. Second Kings 15:5 shows God smites a king with leprosy. I guess it's time for a theology check. God doesn't harm His children in the long run, but if we judge a matter before its time, we may miss what God is doing and end up judging God.

How could Moses deliver Israel out of Egypt if He never went in? God wanted Moses to be born in Egypt, which would have been impossible without Joseph's travail.

Preachers today many times apologize for God, watering down the truth so it will be acceptable, so people will "accept" Jesus, and the church will grow. The truth is what sets people free, and there are very few free people in America. We are given everything, but like Solomon, we entangle ourselves into idolatry so easily, let us pray for hearts like David, the conqueror! David knew when a man came out on the road and cursed him and spit on him that God had a message in it for him; he did not "bind the devil," he knew sovereignty of God (2 Samuel 16:5-14). It is normal not to want to suffer.

In religions where suffering is self-imposed, it is a demonic influence causing people to enter into that so-called "holy" behavior. God knows we don't want suffering, but He orchestrates our lives so that we experience the breaking and being out of control to learn of Him. He never tests us more than we are able to bear. Look at the way God treated his "only begotten son," He submitted himself to the Father, and the Father submitted Him to mankind and demon powers, knowing it was the only way to redeem the elect. The "nerf cross" that is preached today has no suffering; that is why it has no resurrection power. These false prophets say, "Jesus became poor so that you can have a Mercedes." He became poor so that we could be blessed with all spiritual blessings in heavenly places (Ephesians 1:3). In Isaiah 53:10, we see that even God the Father offered His Son on the altar to take away the sins of the world! Now when He takes you through hard times, don't think God has abandoned you or the devil is having his way. God is having His way to conform you to the image of His Son. The false teachers tell only of the blessings, leaving the saints weak and unable to stand in the day of shaking. Count it all joy when you are tried; He is able to bring you through! (James 1:2-4)

TOUGH LOVE

Until a person has been broken by the Holy Spirit and knows the reality of the cross (that the heart is beating and the lungs are pumping only because God Almighty has granted favor for this minute), this person is useless in the service of God and His work on the earth. Jeremiah was taken to the depths of the reality of God's judgment and compassion, seeing Israel fall and yet knowing the love of God was all that any of us really have. The Lord is my portion! (Lamentations 3:24). The fear of the Lord is the beginning of wisdom. The Lord is sovereign, and He needs no one to accomplish His work. People say that God does nothing without man initiating the work in prayers; this is humanistic dung!Nowhere in scripture is man seen as the initiator. In man's search for significance, the carnal mind has ascended to assume an infinite number of deceitful ways of manipulating his place as being one that is "not replaceable." In thought, in philosophy, in business structure, in science, and in every realm of human power struggle, we see evidence of this serpent-like behavior. When the kingdom of God comes upon a person's life, He turns their world upside down! (Acts 17:6) The glory of God becomes their portion and the mantle of their life. The boldness of the Lion of Judah flows through the surrendered and "dead" vessel, confounding the world and producing miracles unexplained by the skeptics. The end-time harvest is beginning, and God will display His glory only through Christians who are dead to ambition and vain glory. Love is the sustaining power that holds a saint through the dark times of breaking and shaking, all faith seems gone at times, and hope is being moved from temporal things to eternal. Only the love of God is left to hold onto in the innermost being; the result of this process is on the other side when all motivation will be in love, not just faith (1 Corinthians 13:2-3, Galatians 5:6).

The problem in our selfish society is people want to experience the resurrection life, the abundant life, without experiencing death and burial. Preachers today are heard all over the nation preaching promises of a healthy, wealthy, and wise life, great crowds gather and pay for books and tapes, but lives aren't changed. Like clouds without rain, these motivational speakers leave out the real gospel. The power of the gospel is only found in the death, burial, and resurrection of Jesus Christ in you. Yes, it is good news, but the bad news comes first; conviction, repentance from dead works and death to self, letting go of the right to be "God," ruling your life, the right to health, wealth, or a wife! (1 Corinthians 15:1-4, Colossians 3:1-4, Romans 12:1-2, 1 Corinthians 6:19-20) The Lord wants to establish His love in us, His character; He wants to live through us. The worst witness—the tackiest people are the selfish, haughty "faith" people, who have manipulated everything around them to possess their dreams. Like "new money," they flaunt what "God has given them," and the world sees right through this façade. Everything that can be shaken will be shaken until all that stands is Christ (Hebrews 12:27). Mathew 7:21-23 proves that even unsaved people can use God's name and His word to get rich and do miracles; therefore, if a man is rich, it doesn't mean he knows God and because a man knows God doesn't mean he is supposed to be rich. Just once, I would like to see a "Faith Church" where the members have more money than the preacher.

Like "candy apples," some of these people look good on the outside, but they are still "rotten to the core." Yes, the Lord does desire to heal people and give them abundance and authority, but not until He has dealt with the heart and brought salvation to the inner man, the body, soul, and Spirit. When we give up on trying to use Jesus to "make our life" and finally "give up our life," then in brokenness, He can work the sanctification necessary for us to become vessels of honor, able to handle the power of the Holy Spirit, and the ambassadorship responsibly. Being rooted and grounded in love, we live in power (1 Corinthians 13). Only a real love of truth and a desire to serve God will bring a person to the point of truly letting go of this life, to move into the eternal Spirit and see with God's perspective.

The flesh says, "Eat, drink and be merry, lest tomorrow we die," "Get all you can now because time is running out."

"Yeah, sure, I love Jesus, but I'll be with Him forever in eternity; now I've got to live it up here, make money, comfort, make a name for myself."

Babylon is raging today, and the major part of the church is engaged with it. The whore of Babylon is a subtle one, like the serpent; the lies are almost truth, so close only the discerning saint can tell the whore from the Bride. We are called to be virgins, wise virgins with our lamps full of oil."The Lord is my portion; fill my cup, oh Lord, your love is better than life."

Stand back and look at the "Christian" landscape as the world sees us. There are thousands of seminars on how to get money, how to be happy, success and self-help. How many seminars do we have on love, gaining wisdom, or being filled with the Spirit? The world knows that Jesus said, "Preach the gospel to the poor, feed the hungry, take care of widows," that is where Jesus is. The lost world quotes 1 Corinthians 13,and the church cannot say a word. When God's people are backsliding and idolaters, God uses the world to rebuke or chasten the Church (Israel). When a person knows Christ, the revelation comes that we were created to serve Him. This is worship. We must have His eternal perspective, only possible through His anointing and the death, burial, and resurrection of our being. People at altars in every church come week after week wanting prayer to "know God's will," God's will is to conform His people into the image of Christ. God's agenda in every redeemed person is to take them through the same life Jesus had. The Word is born in us, then begins the path from proclamation to ruling forever in Him. I call this the "course of the word," and this life of Jesus is the same life all who worship God in Spirit and in truth can expect to experience. When we know God's plan and ways, we will not fight it or lose hope when we face trials or betrayal; we will rejoice in faith, thankful that God has called us to this process of eternal reward. If we delight ourselves in the Lord, He will give us the desires of our hearts, which means He changes our hearts to desire what He desires. Selfish Christians interpret this to mean that if we serve God, He will give us what we want, but He wants to change our desires to match His agenda (Psalm 37:4).

REUNION

Jesus not only brought heaven to earth, but he brought the earth (His Body) up to heaven. We all know about the Anointed One, full of glory being born in a manger, but think, right now in heaven sits flesh and a bone at the right hand of God. In His glorified body, Jesus the Christ, the King of Glory, rules and reigns from heaven. Adam was "of the earth," then God breathed His breath into him (His Spirit, His Glory); this was the union of the Creator and the creation. The fall brought separation through the lie; Adam chose independence. Second Adam came and rejoined the Creator back with the creation by taking on humanity, "the Word became flesh, and we beheld His glory" (John 1:14). Faith, hope, and love, but the greatest of these is love. Only love will sacrifice one's own betterment for the good of others. Faith can possess promises, hope can wait and endure much, but love makes it possible to experience the resurrection life. Positioning yourself as a living sacrifice is the exhortation in Romans 12:1, but this can only be a reality to a believer after he has experienced the love of God. We love Him because He first loved us. People can easily say, "I love God,"but the true test comes when we must give up or sacrifice for Him or others, this is where faith and hope fall short, but love is stronger than death. When we see the vision of the great reunion, we are ready to lay down our temporal lives for the cause of Christ, to see souls saved for eternity. Boldness is a fruit of this reality that we no longer fear man and certainly can no longer enjoy the self-indulgent lifestyle we once did before partaking in the divine nature of God. Faith is the ability to trust God and His promises, but after this comes a reality much greater, one of desiring to give Him all that we have, all that we are, to pour out our being for Him. Seeing the vanity of this life, in all its beauty and splendor, even so, to be able to give to Him, to bring joy to the heart of God, to express back to Him, the gratitude for the love He has shown to us, this is a people prepared for God's use. *The infatuated Bride*, enraptured in His holy love, willing to lay down our lives for Him and the brethren, then the world will know we are His disciples, and He is Lord of all! Oh, there must be more than praying, singing songs, waiting on Him, how can I show God how much I love Him, then he says, "As you have done unto the least of these my brethren, so you have done unto me." If we love God, we will love our brothers and meet the needs of the ones in our world (1 John 3:14-18). In America, this seems so hard because people seem to have all they need; the question today again is, "Who is my neighbor?" In the story Jesus told of the Samaritan, he said anyone in need that you come across is your neighbor. In fear of God, let us repent of these notions that some are called to tend to the poor and needy while others are called to more sophisticated tasks. Come down from your lofty throne, you Laodiceans; we are all called to preach the gospel to every creature, care for the widow and the orphan, and compel them to come in. In fear of God, let us examine our lives and see if we're living the resurrection or just take for granted what Christ has done for us and foolishly squandering our lives away in front of the television.

Go forth, preach the gospel, cast out demons, heal the sick and prophesy in Jesus' name, do all this and more in the power of love!

BUT IT HURTS

"All this talk of death and suffering, I thought the gospel was good news?" The good news comes as a double-edged sword; along with the promises of abundant eternal life, Jesus brought the bad news of death to the carnal man, "Unless you lose your life for my sake, you will not find life eternal." There is a rest for the people of God, a place of peace and joy, adventure and love with the brethren; it is an unpredictable life of spontaneous miracles and excitement, a life of security in God, not temporal things. To enter the rest, we must reckon ourselves dead and let God be God in our lives. By faith, we have the courage to enter into the promises of God, the "Promised Land."When we know God is God, we can let go of all the things that hinder him from living through us. The anointing is such a popular subject and yet so misunderstood. Jesus Christ means "the Anointed One, the Savior." He now lives in the saints,"Christ in you, the hope of glory." In Christ dwells the fullness of the Godhead, and now the fullness of God dwells in us.This was the mystery of the ages, now revealed to the world. The lamb was slain, the veil was *torn*,the circumcised hearts now receive the anointing (Colossians 1:24-27). We only need One Anointing, not many. "The anointing" is enough to heal, preach, discern, teach, love, laugh, cry, do all things (Philippians 4:13). There are many gifts and many manifestations, but only One Anointing. Nowhere in the Word do we see mention of different anointings. The problem is, people's mindsets, traditions, and false teachings hinder the Anointed One from flowing through them to touch the world or the church. We must stop all dead works and be still to learn of the Christ within us. So much "Christian" activity today is frantic flesh trying to do what we see others do or read what some famous preacher did. Only when we hear His voice and get overwhelmed by His Spirit and revelation from the Word will we express outwardly in a true way. We must be free to serve God in the unique way He has formed us to please Him, not copy what others do or conform to a famous preacher's ways; we don't need Saul's armor. We can't work up the anointing; He is already in there; stop trying and start flying! By doing nothing, but receiving, loving God, being loved, all fruit will grow from this; He is the farmer.

All the things we think we need to be happy: cars, career, wife, husband, houses, position, acceptance, and fame, let go of all these and seek first the kingdom of God, be real with the King. Ask for hunger, He will fill you, and then like Jeremiah, you can say, "The Lord is my portion." David said, "Your love is better than life." These prophets knew that death, burial, and resurrection were the key to enter in. God gives us a glimpse of our potential and His destiny for our lives, and then sometimes we are tempted to "make it happen." We see a life that looks good, so we try to create it, name it, claim it, confess it, but after a while, we still aren't happy. The only place of lasting happiness is walking with Christ, even if it's eating beans with hobos. Joseph saw the future in his dreams, but before he would rule, he had to go to the dungeon. We are called to die daily, to rest in Him, to "wait on God," to prove Him. This seems to be a paradox until we experience that what He has for us in the secret placeis better than what we dreamed for anyway. What can compare to the presence of God, His sweet friendship, the unconditional sweet love of Christ when we are caught up in intercourse with him? Enoch walked with God, and never do we read of his ambitions; he chose the best part; like Mary, he saw the beauty of the Lord.

THE ORIGINAL WHO DONE IT MYSTERY

Why did God make the world this way? Or did we make it this way? When we look at the world today and the creation, we must wonder if it is supposed to be like this. Did God intend for the creation to be the way it is, or did man abuse his free will and create the present condition?

Our pre-supposition on this issue will affect every decision in our practical life and is the basis for our Christian philosophy in life, much like our position on the "end of the world" makes some people plant trees and sow for the future, while others sell assets and prepare to escape tribulation or wait for the "any minute now rapture."

Did God know that man would fall in the Garden? Was the fall inevitable because Satan's influence was present in the universe? Did the fall disappoint and shock God, or was it something that he not only foresaw but a necessary event for his eternal purpose to be established? How could God even "allow" it to happen, seeing all the innocent babies and lives that have been affected since that day?

Which came first, the parable or the Lord who told the parables?

Well, the answer is simple: the Lord himself created all things knowing that one day He would come in the flesh and describe the kingdom of God to His disciples using this classroom with all the teaching aids He had built into the creation. Eating and drinking, sowing and reaping, the reality of marriage were all designed into the creation to show us God's ways, His mind for us, and His plan for creation. He is the artist; His entire beautiful universe displays the glory of God. He didn't create it and then decided to make up some analogies from nature to teach us His principles. God designed the creation as a parabolic manifestation of the eternal reality to harvest and train the Sons of God through this dance of life. This truth liberates us to enjoy the abundant life here as well as have hope in our life in eternity.

I rose early in the darkness, a spirit being with a soul and clothes in a body, propelled by a thirst inside. I had to drink the cold, hard liquid, the water, to satisfy the thirst. Why did God make me thirst? Why do I love to drink water? He made us need water as a physical proof, a parable in flesh that we need to partake not only of physical water for our physical body, but we need to drink of the Spirit of God to quench the thirst of our spirit.

Only when we receive this key to interpret the creation can we benefit from all the creation has to offer in teaching us His ways, His purpose in creating us, the fall, and redemption in Christ. The Messiah is the union of the eternal Spirit with the temporal creation, but after Messiah manifests, now part of the creation has become eternal. Flesh and bone are sitting in heaven; this is the mystery of godliness (1 Timothy 3:16). When we can see all of creation as a parable created by God to teach us to "experience," then we no longer fight it or try so hard to change it, but we are free to experience it and learn in it. The wolves surround the lost sheep, and then he cries out until the shepherd comes to his rescue. The wolves can easily kill the lamb, but they are no match for the shepherd. Jesus used His parables often to lead us into the revelation of His creation, His school of parables called life.

Let us trust our lives into the hands of our Creator and die to self that He may raise up into the resurrection life He has destined!

Jesus trusted the Father with His life, and God has raised Him from the dead. All miracles and works that shall not be burned come from this true testing of fire, not the temporal things in this life.

To receive from God, whether it is more of the Spirit or fellowship with Him, we must come to certain death to enter into all He has for us. To lay on the floor and soak in His pretense, we must die to "dead works" and simply receive. In this process, we die to all other opportunities, television, people, pleasures of the world, etc., as we devote a piece of our precious time to Him that we may worship Him by "be-

ing there" with Him. He always rewards us when we seek
Him (Hebrews 11:6).

ANIMALS

Why did God make the animal kingdom? We read in Genesis where He made the heaven, the earth, the plants, the animals, and usually hurry up by all that to start reading about ourselves, man. Have you ever stopped to think, why did God make all these animals in their diversity all over the planet? If it were just for food, he could have made them much easier to eat and probably would not have made them so extravagant in design and behavior. The only reason we cohabit this plant with vicious, beautiful, and delicately strange creatures is that God, by design, wants us to learn revelations of His ways and purpose from them.

The Lion, the king of his realm, displays dominance and authority. The hyenas and vultures represent demons and the powers of darkness, ready to take advantage of the weak, living off the others to survive, as predators with sharp teeth and strength to kill. The only defense of sheep, deer, and other grazers is they have to stick with their group.

Jesus spoke much of sheep and wolves, and there is no better picture of the Body of Christ and the deceiver that feeds off the flock.

But why the peacock in all his pride, the caterpillar with colors to shame the best human designer, why so much diversity, variation, and comic relief? Each kind of animal has its strengths and its weakness. Some forms of wild cattle survive only by warning others of a predator aproaching, leaving any weak family behind they will die. Other groups of cattle, buffalo types, are so bold that in their unity, they are a threat to the lion or tiger, who live to weed out the weak.

What can we, the Body of Christ, the family of God, learn from these? If we lay down our lives for one another and boldly attack the enemy together, we will avoid casualties and have victory. We are all called to preach the gospel and be shepherds to the world and the flock of God. The true shepherd has shown us that the greatest love is to lay down our lives for our friends. Look at all the insects, the fowls of the air, the plants, and how they function and pray for revelation by the Holy Spirit through these things.

When we observe all the beauty, splendor, and sense of humor in the creation, we can only conclude that the Lord is absolutely in control of His creation and generous by nature. Proven by such creatures as dolphins, the lifeguards of the sea, and the angler fish, with His fishing pole and bait built unto His head. The Lord knew that we would grope through the fog of this fallen world and take ourselves too seriously; therefore, He created our surroundings as an infinitely revelatory theatre in which we play the lead role.

Deep in the ocean are extravagantly designed creatures

that have only been seen in modern times, proving God's
never-ending trail of clues.

> But ask the animals, and they will teach you,
> or the birds of the air, and they will tell you;
> or speak to the earth, and it will teach you, or
> let the fish of the sea inform you. Which of all
> these does not know that the hand of the Lord
> has done this? In his hand is the life of every
> creature and the breath of all mankind.

> Job 12:7-10

WHAT'S THE PURPOSE?

What is the purpose of this life? Why are we here? Some days are filled with joy and purpose, others full of questions, problems, and pain! Does God want to fix everything,or is He a cruel guy standing back watching the suffering of the masses while doing nothing about it? There are as many opinions about the questions as there are people, but in America, all the opinions ultimately fit into one of three major categories.

The first one I will briefly explain is the "atheist." The atheist ultimately trusts in reason and "scientific" theory that is usually falsely called "fact" (1 Timothy 6:20). They reason that because we cannot see God or prove that there is a God, then we must explain our existence by our physical surroundings. Many atheists believe in the "theory of evolution," but others do not try to explain it at all and just adopt the philosophy "eat, drink and be merry, lest tomorrow we die." Writers throughout history have all compounded this philosophy. This philosophy basically says, "We are here because of random events in nature, and it does not really make sense, there is no real purpose, so make what you can of it, make it mean something, you are your own god." "Cruel world,""survival of the fittest,""every man for himself,"'"make your own reality," and "intellect is God." The end result of these philosophies is depression, which leads to suicide. If this life is all there is and there is no God, then all we see in nature points to death. The resurrection seen in new trees or plants, for example, would look like endless and impersonal sowing and reaping for the purpose of just keeping this meaningless cycle going. When we die, our body is given back to the earth as fertilizer. With this view, happiness comes when things go well, and hopelessness comes when your "luck" runs out.

Secondly and on the opposite end of the spectrum of the reason is what I will call the "Formula Christians." These people have been quickened by the Holy Spirit and know that there is a God (most of the time). Although superficial in worldview and character, they are very loyal to win the world for Jesus. With all the T-shirts, bumper stickers, and zeal they can muster, they are convinced that God wants everybody in the world to be saved, healed and rich, right now! There is no question about it; God wants all the suffering and problems to stop right now. These "fix-it" mentality people believe that the ball is all in our court, God has done all He is going to do, and now it is up to us to tell everybody about Jesus before it is too late. They preach that it is all "your choice" to go to heaven or hell, so who would choose hell? Somehow they are smarter for "choosing" Jesus, and lost people are dumb or just rebels. Now with this oversimplified version of "the gospel." The nation is full of their "converts" who have now given up because they were not discipled but just talked into being "saved." In trying to be significant, people try to win souls, heal the world, or just anything to prove they are somebody.

The problem with all this is that they can never answer the real questions that their "victims" ask:

- "Why does God let children suffer?"

- "Why do some people that never hear the gospel go to hell?"

- "Why aren't all Christians healthy and rich?"

- "If some people do go to hell, is it our fault because we did not do enough to save them?"

- "Why am I paying for Adam's sin?"

- "Why doesn't life fit into your formulas?"

- "Why are your leaders rich, but you are not?"

- "Why did my faithful grandmother die with some disease?"

God uses these well-meaning, sometimes shallow, and self-righteous Christians in spite of themselves; after all, there are no perfect vessels; only God can make someone saved or healed. By the foolishness of preaching, God has chosen the elect (1 Corinthians 1:21).

Note: This group is called "Formula Christians" because of selfish theology and because "while they should be teaching," they are still desiring "milk" and drinking "formula" (Hebrews 5:11-14).

The third group of people are also very zealous and hold deep convictions about their beliefs, but they have received revelation from the Bible, the Holy Spirit, and by observing the creation.

Knowing that God is God, believing in supernatural healing, miracles, and God prospering saints in what He has called them to do, but also knowing that His ways are above our ways and formulas don't necessarily fit every situation. God's only formula is to form Christ in the saints He has redeemed. After years of trying to get their way with God using "formulas" in vain, this group of believers has learned to be content in whatever state they find themselves in (Philippians 4:11-12). The more mature Christians you talk to know it is impossible to box Him into "always" and "nevers." Through years of the process of sanctification, of working out the salvation of the soul with fear and trembling, these surrendered saints have been convinced by God that he doesn't need us to accomplish His work in the earth; He is sovereign as King of the universe and yet He takes great pleasure in revealing His secrets to His servants and sharing

His work of the harvest with His sons.

Why did God create ornately colored fish at the bottom of the sea doing incredible little mating dances? After all, man did not even discover these until recent technology allowed us to dive thousands of feet below the surface and bring back photographs of these spectacular little creatures. Did He make all the infinite detail and beauty of His creation so that public television would have good footage to try to sell us on evolution? Doesn't all the flamboyance of the birds' splendid colors or the fish's light spectrum become a little overdone when we consider all the starving babies in Africa?

If God is frantic about trying to fix everything, how can we enjoy the beauty of His creation that so justly gives Him glory? He created all this so that we might learn of His ways, to know love and faith. Did the caterpillars begin to make cocoons and resurrect as butterflies after Jesus went to the cross, or was that just another part of the creation design from the beginning of time to silently scream to us the purpose of God? Selah! God, the artist, loves to create, He loves to love, He loves for us to discover His grand plan, the butterfly, the cow, the dung beetle, all love to serve Him and help secure us in love, on our path to glory!

It has been said many times that "man creates God in his own image." In America, we have the "American dream," "a beautiful house and cars, a beautiful wife and children, and, of course, money to travel and what would all this be without health to enjoy it." We tend to turn God into a "genie," where we make wishes in the form of confessing and claiming and coveting all these things to build our own little kingdom.

In third world countries, Christians see God as Savior, provider, healer, whatever the most urgent need is at the time, and God is all these. Whether here, where we have it all or there where they have less, we all tend to develop the "fix it" mentality, but what we need is the "mind of Christ," where Paul said, "Whether I have much or have little, I have learned to be content in all things" (Philippians 4:11-12). The only things we are exhorted to covet are the Spirit, the spiritual gifts, and the prosperity of our brethren (Hebrews 13:5, 1 Timothy 6:6-11).

The lesson God wants us to learn is love, how to prefer our brother, love our neighbor, and love our enemies; everything else is God's job and will fall into place. All the stress and anxiety about time running out or "we aren't doing enough for God" simply melts away when we realize the revelation that God is in control and the whole creation is progressing according to plan, even the harvest of man (Hebrews 2:15). The fix-it mentality is adverse to our being, always thinking that God is frantic about fixing everything, saving everyone before it's too late, and time can somehow elude God.

When we finally see that the Lord *is* God, then we are free to "enjoy the mess" while at the same time move with compassion to reach people in the love of God, now in a quality way, not a frantic rush. Until we enter the rest, we don't learn from the creation.

God manifests this whole creation for His elect in which to have a training ground to learn and grow. The fall, the redemption,and the sanctification process of believers were all part of the plan. He created it, He cursed it, and He resurrected it in love, proving that God is the only hero. Jesus, the man, even said over and over, "There is no one good but God." He was saying that only the Spirit will last. The other alternative is that the fall and wickedness of man shocked God, so He had to come out with "plan B," call 911, and send His Son to redeem man and bring healing, to "fix" everything. Christians' beliefs on these issues will determine their philosophy of life and their predisposition to the character of God. In trying to make God palatable, nice, and "believable," people reject the fact that God wanted the fall to take place. The problem is our perspective is limited, and we can sometimes forget that the destruction of our flesh can bring eternal fruit in the spirit, as proven by God slaying His Son on the cross or Paul putting Hymenaeus and Alexander out of the church for the saving of their souls (1 Timothy 1:20).

I am persuaded that God's sovereignty sees to it that ministers of healing believe that God wants all healed right now. Evangelists believe that God wants all saved right now, etc., but theologians that see the big picture and strengthen the body through great times of tribulation know the deeper truths of God's sovereignty and His eternal purposes. Some argue that God does not make anyone sick, that "sickness does not come from God,"but He created all things, and foreknowledge alone will not "let God off the hook" for being responsible for all things, after all. Everyone believes that God has foreknowledge;but why did He put Adam and Eve in the Garden with the serpent? Neither Adam nor his wife were any match for the serpent. Lucifer fell before "the creation was made subject to vanity" (Romans 8:20), and God knew that he would beguile the woman. This was all done for our learning; the law cannot produce life, "don't eat of this and do eat of that" is not the "more excellent way."

The Spirit gives life, but only a resurrected being can possess the fullness of the Spirit, the eternal purpose of God is to produce a faithful Bride for eternity to sit on the throne with Him after He has brought us from the fall, the ashes, the pit and breathed into us His eternal Spirit, we know the difference in being independent and being dependent, in love with Him, re-united. The angels were created and saw God in the Spirit; they chose independence. We are born again; we will never rebel in heaven. As beings born into the fall then called out of the world by the Creator, we receive the light and know the pit we are lifted from; we see His face and never want to go back! Only redeemed creatures can know this. Satan challenged God one day, and God said, "Consider Job." God did not have to enter the argument, but He enjoyed spoiling Satan. God said, "Consider Job" because of what we see in Job 2:10, "Why should we love and serve God only for good, shall we not accept the bad as well?" Oh, that modern Christians would have this heart, then we will see true revival and harvest, more importantly, a true representation of the true God! God has desired a Bride to represent Him, to think as He thinks, to know His real purpose for ages. What joy it brings a man's heart when his wife knows what he is thinking, his deepest convictions. This is what every man truly wants.

The future of the church holds great promise, for we are moving toward the day when our doctrine will come from lovers of truth who will present the Word of God in its fullness and not be afraid to question what has been taught. We have seen twisted theology to sell the "faith" preacher's bill of goods, and we have seen twisted theology to control masses of people under a false priesthood called "the Roman Catholic church." Now there are multitudes of underground believers full of revelation who know that liberty is the rule of God, and we are saying, "Give me liberty or give me death!"

God wants to take us through the storms, darkness, and the fire, where it feels like hell, to work faith into us, where it seems there is no reason for faith. We can go "beyond reason" only by the Spirit. Why do we think that Job had a hard life, but ours should be easy? If we go through what Job did, losing all, even health, and see that the Lord is all we need, then we can never be tempted again with worldly things, fame, fortune, or pleasure.

TO THE CHURCH OF THE SELF-RIGHTEOUS OR A LETTER TO GOD'S FAVOR-ITES

"For who makes you differ from another?And what do you have that you did not receive? Now if you did indeed receive it, why do you boast as if you had not received it?" (1 Corinthians 4:7)

The Body of Christ longs to fulfill it;s destiny on the earth and please our Lord Jesus Christ. Saints pray continually, "Lord, let Your will be done, show us your ways, please save the lost, our families, and heal our land." These prayers can be heard at church meetings all around the world, but there is a major stumbling block to the realization of these desires.The problem is that the Church is self-righteous! Just ask the world how they perceive Christians. Do they answer, "Oh, these people are so humble; they love each other"? No, they say, "The Church is a bunch of hypocrites." We all know this is used as an excuse, but it was *never* said of Jesus. The common attitude in the body of Christ today is, "We don't need more doctrine. No more theology! We just need a relationship!"Let us examine this subtle scheme of the

71

serpent to hinder growth in the Body of Christ.Do we need deeper relationships? Yes, of course, but the truth frees us to experience deeper relationships.When our ears are closed to foundational teaching that has the power to challenge our thinking, the house is not built on the rock of Christ.

Peter writes, "Grace and peace be multiplied to you in the knowledge of God and of Jesus our Lord" (2 Peter 1:2). We see here that knowledge of God, the Father, produces grace and peace, and grace is the revelation that the Church still needs today.Many churches use the word "grace" on their signs, but they don't truly understand what it means."Grace" in Hebrew comes from "chen," which means "favor" or "to bestow,"which comes from a word meaning "to stoop over." The New Testament mentions grace; the Greek "charis" means "gift." Grace is given; it is a gift. Grace means favor, and if everyone were given favor, it would no longer be "favor."Most Christians have taken a big dose of the leaven of the Pharisees; they said things like, "I fast twice a week.I tithe on all my stuff; God, I thank you that I'm not like those evil sinners." But many Christians today think,"Thank you, Lord, I'm not one of those who drink too much, beat their wives, and only go to church on Easter."

Paul received the mystery of grace long before the other apostles; born out of season, he said,"I am what I am by the grace of God."Paul understood that he would still be a murderer if the Lord of glory had not come to him, struck

him from his horse so lovingly, and "called" him into the
kingdom of light.

> But the Lord said to him, "Go, for he is a cho-
> sen vessel of Mine to bear My name before
> Gentiles, kings, and the children of Israel.For I
> will show him how many things he must suffer
> for My name's sake."

Acts 9:15-16

Here we see the Lord's call on Saul. We must see this
revelation to know that God is for us; saving us was His plan
all along, and saving others is His plan, as well.

The striving we see in the church today to beg and con-
vince God to do things for us, to "help" us win souls, and
to show His glory in the earth, is the fruit of the humanistic
stronghold in the minds of modern man. Our real call is to
reckon ourselves dead, alive unto God, and to receive the
revelation and to know, "For we are His workmanship created in Christ Jesus unto good works, which God hath before ordained that we should walk in them" (Ephesians 2:10,
KJV).Until the born-again believers understand that we did
absolutely *nothing*to be saved, then we are still self-righteous."Blessed is the nation whose God is the Lord, The people He has chosen as His own inheritance" (Psalm 33:12).

In 1 Corinthians 1:2, the Word says that we are sanctified

73

in Christ Jesus and called to be saints (paraphrased). The word "sanctified" means "set apart."Jesus, the chief shepherd, has set us apart from the world.A little lamb cannot find its way to the shepherd; rather, the shepherd must find and save the lost sheep.

Parables are spiritual truths, formed into the creation, part of God's design that we may know the heart of God. God chose to use the parable of birth to show us the picture of our regeneration.We did not choose to be born the first time, and we didn't choose to be born-again either.We were birthed by God and the faithful servants He used to bring us in. Most Christians today believe that they made a good "decision," based on the information at hand, and "accepted" Jesus into their hearts. The Bible clearly states that all believers were born by the will of God, not by the will of man."Who were born, not of blood, nor of the will of the flesh, nor of the will of man, but of God"(John 1:13). Like an adopted child taken from familiar surroundings, we kick and scream when our Father strips away the things we depend on: friends, position, even our righteousness.Only after time has passed, we see His faithful love and know that He brought us out of the darkness into His kingdom of light.

This truth is again seen in Romans 9:16 (KJV),"So then it is not of him that willeth, nor of him that runneth, but of God that sheweth mercy."Romans 9:18, "Therefore He has mercy on whom He wills, and whom He wills He hard-

ens."This scripture challenges all we hear in today's humanistic society.The truth will absolutely slay the carnal mind,
which is the enemy of God, according to Romans 8:7, and
leave us with no glory of our own."That no flesh should glory in his presence"(1 Corinthians 1:29, KJV). As long as the
Christian thinks he chose to be saved, "accepted" Jesus, or
made an intellectual decision, he cannot really understand or
humbly rejoice that his name is written in the Lamb's Book
of Life (Luke 10:20[b], paraphrased).We don't rejoice about
something we earn; we rejoice in the love of God that is giv-
en over and over again.Even though we fall short of our calling, He is steadfast and gentle to keep us.We are kept by the
power of God.We are chosen by God. Read 1 Corinthians
1:21-31 and see that the Jews require a sign, the Greeks seek
wisdom, and yet, in 1 Corinthians 1:24, 27 (KJV), God says,
"But unto them which are called, both Jews and Greeks,
Christ is the power of God, and the wisdom of God." "But
God hath chosen the foolish things of the world to confound
the wise; and God hath chosen the weak things of the world
to confound the things which are mighty."We see in these
two scriptures that both Jews and Greeks stumble, but if you
are called, you will see the light.I realize that this controversy is not new, but the end-time Bride of Christ is receiving
this revelation to have the strength to endure. John 15:16,
"You did not choose Me, but I chose you…"

THE LIE

Satan has sown the lie of "self" so deep into mankind; only the revelation of Christ by the Holy Spirit can free us to be able to see that God wants us saved and victorious, even more than we want that for ourselves. It all started in the Garden. Actually, it all started when Lucifer said, "I will ascend above the heights of the clouds, I will be like the Most High"(Isaiah 14:14). After being cast down, he went to the Garden and said to Eve, "You will be like the Most High." Satan saw that trying to be God cost him all that he had. Satan then wanted to bring man down with him, so he went for Eve. This, wanting to be God, is the mystery of iniquity. Man ate of the tree of knowledge of good and evil, and evil religion is still going strong, keeping the majority of people from Christ. Man in control, with God involved as his ritual only, is Antichrist. God wants to be in every area of our life, not only His name used on our rituals.

> Let no one deceive you by any means; for that Day will not come unless the falling away comes first, and the man of sin is revealed, the son of perdition, who opposes and exalts himself above all that is called God or that is worshiped, so that he sits as God in the temple of God, showing himself that he is God. For

the mystery of lawlessness is already at work;
only He who now restrains will do so until He
is taken out of the way.

2 Thessalonians 2:3-4

Millions of people meet every week all over the world and sing songs "I want to be like you, Lord." We hear teachings about how to be like God. That is evidence that the leaders are missing the point. We will never be like Jesus. We must die to self that Christ may be formed in us:"My little children of whom I travail in birth again until Christ be formed in you" (Galatians4:19, KJV). Our whole secular culture is trying to be like God without God! Watch the latest celebrities and influentials of the world; the spirit they walk in is: to be good, to do good, and to be as gods. Behavioral Christianity is the most popular idea today in the church and in the world.That is why the church is powerless. When we know the truth of the gospel, then we will do greater works than Jesus did (John 14:12), but with much persecution. Why is there no persecution today in America? Because the true gospel is rarely preached!

THE TRUTH

Paul's gospel, the one with power, brings an absolute death to the flesh. Jesus is called the "rock of offense" because you can't add Jesus to your life, you must lose your life to find it. We are buried in baptism.This is not just a cute ceremony; it is death. Not only the fact that we are dead and hid in Christ,but we die daily that the Christ may live and work through us. "For you died, and your life is hidden with Christ in God" (Colossians 3:3). To "reckon ourselves dead" is the expectation to all believers endeavoring to bring forth fruit. This is the resurrection of life! In Hebrews 6:1, we see the principles of the doctrine of Christ. The first step is repentance from dead works. In this doctrine, we find our death. Most people believe this refers to the old covenant sacrifice and law, but the concept here is much deeper. Repentance comes from the word "metanoeo," which means a transformation of the mind, to reconsider, a change in our minds about what makes us right with God...righteousness.

The Bible says that God makes us the righteousness of God in Christ (2 Corinthians 5:21). Most Christians think that repent means telling God we're sorry about sin.That is confession, not repentance. In Acts 2:38, Peter, a Jew, was preaching to Jews who came to Jerusalem for Pentecost. He said, "Repent."He was not saying "to be sorry for your sin" but to "change their minds about righteousness. Oh, and about the man that you crucified fifty-three days ago, he was the Messiah!" Then in Acts 2:39, Peter says, "For the promise is to you and to your children, and to all who are afar off, as many as the Lord our God will call." In the old covenant, "repent" means "to return" because the Jews were with God but then left, seeking after idols. In the New Testament, "repent" means "to change your self-righteous outlook of thinking," like "I'm a good person" and receive the love of the truth. God has done it all through His Son's death on the cross. "Repent" to the Jews was a call to turn back by changing their minds about righteousness. "Repent" to people now is a call to change our minds about how to be righteous before God, and the call is to all walks of life; most have never been with God.

Grace is the ability to experience a supernatural event. Salvation is only possible through supernatural ability (grace) to confess unto salvation that Jesus is Lord. Romans 10:9 proves that God must initiate each individual salvation. People think the gospel and grace are out there in the air (omnipresent), and God is waiting for them to choose. In Titus 2:11, where he says that salvation has appeared into the men, he refers to God manifest in the earth; not that grace is automatically extended to all. Only when God quickens a person individually can they believe in their heart and confess unto salvation. Each person who is saved is a unique and personal work by the God Almighty, an individual "enablement" unto eternal life.

"But God, who is rich in mercy, for his great love wherewith he loved us, Even when we were dead in sins, hath quickened us together with Christ, (by grace ye are saved)" (Ephesians 2:4-5, KJV).

Beloved, a dead man does not make a decision and has no power to make himself alive. We cannot even ask God to save us without faith, and we would not know the need to be saved without the conviction of the Holy Spirit. We receive faith when we are quickened.

> I am crucified with Christ:nevertheless I live;
> yet not I, but Christ liveth in me: and the life
> which I now live in the flesh I live by the faith
> of the Son of God, who loved me, and gave
> himself for me.I do not frustrate the grace of
> God: for if righteousness come by the law, then
> Christ is dead in vain.
>
> Galatians 2:20-21(KJV)

As the gospel is preached, the Word of faith is planted in a person, and simultaneously the Holy Spirit quickens. Then, and only then, we confess unto salvation, "Oh, Jesus is Lord!"Like Mary, we just say okay. The Word is planted, the Holy Spirit waters, Christ is born in us, and we exchange lives with Jesus Christ. Read Luke 1:28-38 and Mathew 1:18-25 and discover that man had little choice in these matters. When God sent an angel to tell Mary what was going to happen, He offered her no choice.

> But what saith it? The word is nigh thee, even in thy mouth, and in thy heart: that is, the word of faith, which we preach; That if thou shalt confess with thy mouth the Lord Jesus, and shalt believe in thine heart that God hath raised him from the dead, thou shalt be saved. For with the heart man believeth unto righteousness; and with the mouth confession is made unto salvation.

> Romans 10:8-10 (KJV)

God initiates the work. "Being confident of this very thing, that he which hath begun a good work in you, will perform it until the day of Jesus Christ" (Philippians 1:6, KJV).

Like Abraham, we acknowledge that He is Lord and are counted righteous, not of dead works, but by trusting in the work of the Lamb on the cross. The Father accepts us through the blood of His Son, proven by the Holy Spirit. The notion of our "accepting" Him is preposterous.

The first "dead works" were done by Adam and his wife when they made garments out of fig leaves. God gently showed them a more excellent way: sacrifice! They must have felt a little offended when He did not accept their "works," but not as offended as Cain felt when his works were rejected. Cain had no excuse when we conclude that Adam told his son about the first sacrifice: when God covered the original sin with the blood and skins of an animal. Abel received the revelation of sacrifice and pleased God. These two remnants have lived on throughout history. Babel was the epitome of Antichrist works, and today we see the "new Babylon" being manifest. The point here, however, is portrayed vividly through Jacob and Esau. In Romans 9, we see the best picture of the election. In verses 11-12, it says,

> For the children, being not yet born, neither
> having done any good or evil, that the purpose
> of God according to election might stand, not
> of works, but of him that calleth; it was said
> unto her, the elder shall serve the younger.

Romans 9:11-12 (KJV)

This whole chapter is necessary to reveal the heart of God "all Israel is not Israel." God has designed His creation with some principles that are difficult to understand. We are transformed from the kingdom of darkness into the kingdom of light, then begins the transformation by the renewing of our mind.

I beseech you, therefore, brethren, by the mercies of God, that you present your bodies a living sacrifice, holy, acceptable to God, which is your reasonable service.And do not be conformed to this world, but be transformed by the renewing of your mind, that you may prove what is the good and acceptable and perfect will of God.

Romans 12:1-2

The spirit of the world today says, "All dogs go to heaven," but most people really believe that all people should go to heaven. This makes sense to our carnal minds.Reality comes, however, when we begin to see things God's way. Isaiah 43:4(KJV) says, "Since thou wast precious in my sight, thou hast been honorable and I have loved thee: therefore will I give men for thee, and people for thy life."When God commands Joshua to go into the Promised Land and take dominion, he was commanded to kill all those evil Satan worshippers. Joshua was not told to hand out nice gospel tracts. If degenerate people were not wiped out when God brought judgment, we would never have had the opportunity to live. God's ways are higher than our ways.

FAVOR-ITES

Israel was God's chosen in the old covenant time. This relationship was a shadow of things to come. Christians today easily accept the fact that God had a "chosen" people in Israel but struggle with a "chosen" people now. Hebrews 13:8 says that God does not change. In Romans 9, Paul writes of Pharaoh; God extends mercy upon whom He will. Aren't you glad God has shown mercy to you? When it says God hardened pharaoh's heart, we must realize that God did not need to touch pharaoh's heart with "hardener," He simply turned up the heat of circumstances. Pharaoh was in the Adamic nature, and hatred is the fruit. God plucks some out of the fire and leaves others in, He has mercy on whom He has mercy, and no one "deserves" it. Today he says all Israel is not Israel. Romans 9:6 says, "But it is not that the word of God has taken no effect. For they are not all Israel who are of Israel. "Some people from every nation, tribe, and language will be saved exactly like the Lord sovereignly orchestrates it, to be His holy nation, peculiar people, His church, the royal priesthood. Only when we see and accept this truth can we give God all the glory and rejoice that our names are written in the Lamb's Book of Life from the foundation of the world.

The beast that you saw was, and is not, and
will ascend out of the bottomless pit and go
to perdition. And those who dwell on the earth
will marvel, whose names are not written in
the Book of Life from the foundation of the
world, when they see the beast that was, and is
not, and yet is.

Revelation 17:8

When Jesus said these words to His disciples, "Rejoice
not that the demons are subject to you, but rejoice that your
name is written in the Lamb's Book of Life," He was making
it clear that they were chosen to be with Him forever. When
this day comes in a believer's life, He can finally cease from
dead works and all fear of losing His salvation. Salvation is
not ours to find or lose; it is the person of Jesus Christ, God
manifests in the flesh, and He loses no one. We are kept by
the power of God. In the old covenant, we conclude God
saved some while others were left."Jesus Christ is the same
yesterday, today, and forever" (Hebrews 13:8). A young
Jewish boy had little choice in being born into a family that
was saved on Passover.

FREE WILL

Now, let us deal with the concept of freewill. Adam was walking with God, free and full of glory. Adam had freewill to obey God or disobey God. When he chose to buy the serpent's lie, he lost freewill for all of us. In Adam, all died, but in Christ the second Adam, all are made alive."For as in Adam all died, even so in Christ all shall be made alive"(1 Corinthians 15:22). When a person is regenerated by the Holy Spirit (made alive in Christ), their freewill is reinstituted. This explains why some Christians witness to people and shake their heads in disbelief when someone rejects Christ. "It's so easy, just believe, ask Jesus into your heart, and go to heaven," they say. These zealous ones do not realize that no one comes to Jesus unless the Father draws them in His time. The word "choose" is found in the Bible, but never does God speak this word to the lost or to those who are not in covenant with Him already. "Blessed is the man whom thou choosest, and causest to approach unto thee, that he may dwell in thy courts: we shall be satisfied with the goodness of thy house, even of thy holy temple"(Psalm 65:4, KJV).So, why are we so surprised when the flesh rejects God? Paul said, "There is no good thing in me, in my flesh that is." Only when the living God quickens the spirit are we able to receive the love of truth and confess unto salvation? When born-again leaders fall, it is only evidence that they have not been walking in the Spirit but instead fulfilling the lust of the flesh. We must get over the shock at the wickedness of the flesh. We all know how selfish our own flesh is. Only when we accept this will the lost see us as humble and thankful, the redeemed.

We do not know who will be saved or when. Therefore, we must preach the gospel to every creature but not with an attitude that it is all up to them.

"And when the Gentiles heard this, they were glad, and glorified the word of the Lord: and as many as were ordained to eternal life believed" (Acts 13:48, KJV).

> And a certain woman named Lydia, a seller
> of purple, of the city of Thyatira, which wor-
> shipped God, heard us: whose heart the Lord
> opened, that she attended unto the things which
> were spoken of Paul.

Acts 16:14 (KJV)

People who are dead in trespasses are slaves to sin (Romans 6:18-20). We, the redeemed, are slaves to righteousness. We must gently but boldly share the truth in love with lost people. Some plant, others water, but God gives the increase. Unless we abide in Him, we bring forth no fruit. God is sovereign, and He uses people where they are. We do not have to be doctrinally perfect to win the lost, but the more revelation we have, the more we can worship God in spirit and in truth. Our life is for worship, not just when we are in the church building. Our freewill as born-again believers is exercised in our daily choosing to serve God by serving others, not ourselves. The exhortation to us is to walk in the Spirit and not fulfill the lust of the flesh. Only when we know that God initiated our redemption are we in the right perspective to serve God from a true motive.We, unlike the cults, are not winning souls to earn approval from God or get our own planet, but the love of God constrains us to do so.All glory to God.

THE CONTROVERSY

This controversy of election and predestination has been debated for centuries. Satan always subtly perverts the most life-changing doctrines. He knows that if people know the truth, he is unarmed. The Church has dealt with this by "roping off" certain doctrines as divisive and not dealing with them for the sake of unity. Well, God chose Paul, Peter, and John to deal with these issues, and their epistles became canonized scripture. The carnal mindset is "let's take the path of least resistance." The enemy distorts truth causing division. The Pharisees, "the separatists," were a perversion of the truth of election. John the Baptist said, "Think not to say we are children of Moses [in other words, don't believe you are some special people because of your great-grandfathers' religion with God], but bring forth fruit of repentance" (brackets added for clarity). The truth is sovereign grace or election; as it is sometimes called causes a Son of God to be ever humble and have no confidence in the flesh. Satan tries to bring the opposite effect. The effect of this truth in a person's life depends on whether the revelation is mixed with the Holy Spirit's love, bringing forth humility and thanksgiving, or mixed with the carnal nature, bringing forth pride and the Pharisee spirit. Most churches and denominations that believe in election and predestination are dead and separatist. No part of the body has it all. The charismatic camp is strong in the gifts and live worship but very weak in doctrine. The traditional old denominations are "dead" because this revelation was not mixed with zeal. Reformation came forth as a result of revelation, received by men of faith such as Martin Luther and John Calvin; this "Reformed Theology" was the beginning of church renewal; all these men believed strongly in sovereign grace and election. The controversy of who initiates salvation and the possibility of a person losing his salvation was an issue even in the early church. In all the epistles, the theme of God's sovereignty was emphasized to combat the antichrists of the day and establish believers in the truth of God's sustaining power. We are kept by the power of God. The "Works Mentality" was sown again after the apostles died, and the Roman Catholic Church exploited the lie until the Reformation, then Reformed Theology brought liberty. Today the battle still rages, the truth versus the lie.

THE BIG PICTURE

Throughout church history, we see a battle against the church; the enemy works to exaggerate and distort, to prevent balance and unity. Jesus said, "God is a Spirit: and they that worship him must worship him in spirit and in truth"(- John 4:24, KJV). The Early Church, the apostolic beginning of the church, started as a balanced body of believers.

> And they continued steadfastly in the apostles' doctrineand fellowship, in the breaking of bread, and in prayers. Then fear came upon every soul, and many wonders and signs were done through the apostles.
>
> Acts 2:42-43

The Church had solid teaching and theology mixed with manifestations of the Spirit and the charismatic reality. The Church today is divided. Unity is the cry, but many leaders want to unite by compromise. God will not allow His remnant to compromise. On the one hand, we see churches that are strong in the Spirit; these move in the gifts and lead in the live worship movement but are weak in theology. On the other hand, the seminary-fed bible churches and major denominations are strong in the truth of the Word but very weak in the revelation of the Holy Spirit, and their services

93

are "dead." Today we are at the threshold of the apostolic manifestation of the end-time Bride, where the Lord is raising up new "Davids" to proclaim the truth that will bring the body into true unity, in Spirit, and in truth! First, the filling of God's people with the revelation of God's love, denominational walls will continue to come down in this mighty outpouring of the Spirit. We are learning to "be filled" together. Next, we will see a generation of new teachers speaking with authority, the oracles of God. Teaching the corporate body the truth of Christ and His purpose from Genesis to Revelation unashamed of the gospel and unafraid to deal with "hard sayings." "Sauls," who cling to tradition and safe teaching, must repent or retire because God is jealous of His people, and He will set us free here on earth!

It is a new day! The end-time Bride has the best of all the camps put together, to be unstoppable. From the faith movement, we know we can prosper and rule in the marketplace; from the charismatic renewal, we know worship and the gifts of the spirit, and from Reformed Theology, we know who we are in Christ, unshakeable by the devils lying tongue of accusation and condemnation. Going to the altar week after week to get saved again only proves that Satan can still tell people that they have not done enough or they aren't pleasing to God. We can never do enough; that is why the Lamb was slain before the foundation of the world to show us God's infinite love and provide our salvation with no chance of failure. "All who dwell on the earth will worship him, whose names have not been written in the Book of Life of the Lamb slain from the foundation of the world"(Revelation 13:8).When we focus on what He has done, we will accomplish more. In any relationship, when we focus on the other person, and they focus on us, this promotes growing intercourse.

Let us press into God by faith to receive more of His gracious love, knowing we are accepted through the blood of the lamb without shame and go forth, proclaiming the works of God, for He is the Creator, the Redeemer, and the faithful husband throughout eternity. Nothing or nobody can stop God and His plan to display His glory!

> Yet in all these things we are more than conquerors through Him who loved us. For I am persuaded that neither death nor life, nor angels nor principalities nor powers, nor things present nor things to come, nor height nor depth, nor any other created thing, shall be able to separate us from the love of God which is in Christ Jesus our Lord.

> Romans 8:37-39

WHY

What if God, wanting to show His wrath and to make His power known, endured with much longsuffering, the vessels of wrath prepared for destruction, and that He might make known the riches of His glory on the vessels of mercy, which He had prepared beforehand for glory, even us whom He called, not of the Jews only, but also of the Gentiles?

Romans 9:22-24

HARVEST

The perspective we must receive on the plan of salvation is seen in James 5:7:

> Be patient therefore, brethren, unto the coming
> of the Lord. Behold, the husbandman waiteth
> for the precious fruit of the earth, and hath long
> patience for it, until he receive the early and
> latter rain.

James 5:7(KJV)

The Creator of the universe is a husbandman who planted this vineyard in faith, expecting a good harvest. I don't need to prove that God is successful in all that He does; this is quite obvious to us all. The celebration in heaven will not be compromised by saints lamenting over their friends who didn't choose Jesus because we didn't pray enough, or we didn't witness enough;we could never do enough. In heaven, we will all see from God's perspective. While it is still called today, let us serve God fervently, for He desires to use us.

Adam means "of the earth," the first man was of the earth, then God breathed the spirit into him. The second Adam was from above:"The first man was of the earth, made of dust; the second Man is the Lord from heaven"(1 Corinthians 15:47).

97

Jesus took on the creation to harvest us from the vineyard. Paul spoke of this as being a sort of firstfruits; the early church was the first harvest. In Revelation 13:8(KJV),"And all that dwell upon the earth shall worship him [beast], whose names are not written in the book of life of the Lamb slain from the foundation of the world" (brackets added for clarity). We see that those that are "of the world" are bound to follow the beast (Greek word for "world" here is earth), but those who have been born from above follow the Lamb, the quickening spirit:"And so it is written, the first man Adam was made a living soul; the last Adam was made a quickening spirit" (1 Corinthians 15:45, KJV). God has sown His word into good soil and is reaping a harvest. The whole creation is going according to God's plan, a vineyard equipped with trials and tests to perfect His Bride.

The perspective that will set us free is when we realize we are "here for the ride"; we are not in control, He created us, He redeemed us, and we are secure in His hands. Like a damsel screaming from the tower of the castle, our knight in shining armor has come to our rescue.So many Christians today emphasize the devil and his power and influence. He can do nothing to the redeemed except what the Father allows for our perfecting. Peace is found in knowing that the Lord is God. Satan's biggest tactic is to exaggerate his power; like a mosquito with a big mouth, he screams in the ears of saints, accusing us, accusing God, until we give in and step out of the secret place and take our life back into our own hands. The three Hebrews in Nebuchadnezzar's furnace knew God's sovereign faithfulness. Knowing the truth enough to die for Him, they subjected themselves to the altar of fire, knowing that God knew their situation. Now we know God orchestrated it for His glory and our learning.

WHO IS IN CONTROL?

Man has learned to control his environment. Through air conditioning systems, man controls the atmosphere of living spaces; with firearms, man can control great numbers of people, and with economic manipulation, backed by nuclear threat, rulers seemingly control continents. Humanistic philosophy promotes man controlling his eternal destiny by choice. This has crept into the church, causing much confusion. In reality, man does not control his destiny. God orchestrates the affairs of man. The footsteps of the righteous are ordered by the Lord (Proverbs 16:9). The redeemed saints of God are exhorted to seek those things that are above.

> If then you were raised with Christ, seek those things which are above, where Christ is, sitting at the right hand of God. Set your mind on things above, not on things on the earth. For you died, and your life is hidden with Christ in God.
>
> Colossians 3:1-3

As born-again Christians, we do walk in a relationship with the living God, and He leaves much of our destiny to our own level of faith and how much we act on His word.

101

"According to your faith be it unto you." By obedience, we possess all our inheritance in Christ or shrink back into unbelief and crawl into heaven as by fire. But never does the Bible speak of us initiating salvation. Once we're saved, we are sons, and our inheritance is very exciting. The world, on the other hand, those of the earth are at the mercy of the god of this world.

"For God hath put in their hearts to fulfill his will, and to agree, and give their kingdom unto the beast, until the words of God shall be fulfilled"(Revelation 17:17, KJV).

We see here who is in control absolutely! Control is the issue. We have psychologists using this buzzword. The United Nations is gaining power to control the world. Technology is advancing to control the people of the earth, but we need not fear; our Father is in control! The reason this concept is so hot now is that God has boiled this issue up to the surface. As we draw closer to the end of days, more and more of the war between light and darkness will be revealed. As kingdom is divided against kingdom, the Holy Spirit is dealing with every person on the planet to bring about the manifestation of the sons of God. The purpose of these modern epistles is not to stir controversy or excuse saints into lethargy. The purpose is to exhort believers to let go of their own righteousness and let God be God. He started this place;He will accomplish His plan. Give glory where glory is due. In humility, we compel the lost to receive the promise

102

of the ages. To any person living on the earth today, I plead with you to repent (change your mind about righteousness), seek truth to know if you are in the faith, to know if your name is written in the Lamb's Book of Life!

> But we are bound to give thanks always to God for you, brethren beloved of the Lord, because God hath from the beginning chosen you to salvation through sanctification of the Spirit and belief of the truth: whereunto He called you by our gospel, to the obtaining of the glory of our Lord Jesus Christ.
>
> 2 Thessalonians 2:13-14

SUPPRESSING THE TRUTH (ROMANS 1:18)

We are born into a runaway train; the world is going down an old course, a rut well-worn by centuries of tradition which all started first with Adam, then with Israel, and finally with the first coming of Christ and the establishment of the church. A great awakening took place at the Reformation, but today we are at the threshold of the greatest awakening ever experienced by man. We need revolution today in the hearts, minds, and actions of man. The stage is set like never before for an instant sweeping of change in the minds of the world. God has now made it possible through technology to have the whole world witness an event together. The world is now one small community. Therefore, truth, revelation, and even error can be consumed by everyone simultaneously at any given moment. God is Spirit, and He does not need technology to accomplish His work, but we are all witnessing events simultaneously. All over the world today, the enlightened ones are all receiving revelation of God's truth, His ways, and a glimpse of events that are about to unfold. Kingdom is diving against kingdom. The people who will die for truth and want to live for truth are opposed to the people who love power and money. Christ in the saints is at war with Satan in the goats: man is Antichrist when he tries to be God. The original sin was to "be like God" it's nothing new. Today you are either dying to your selfishness and Christ is loving through you, or you are striving to get your way, and that makes you part of the problem. We live in the "Information Age," and the war is raging on how to get the truth out. God hates those who suppress the truth, therefore oppressing the people for selfish gain (Romans 1:18). The conspiracy goes much deeper than the Illuminati, Russia hoax, globalism, Chinagate, Watergate, or JFK. The conspiracy started when Lucifer fell, and he knew the glory of God; now, his passion was to hide the glory of God from man; envy was his driving force. Throughout the ages, Satan has tried to hide the truth of God's plan from man by perverting our image of God through lies and religious institutions. In the death, burial, and resurrection of Jesus Christ, God spoiled Satan (fallen Lucifer), and now when we are brought to the "secret place," the "dead zone," hid in Christ, wetoo, know God as He really is and walk in supernatural trust and loyalty to our Creator, Redeemer, and Husband. Jesus Christ, the great liberator, has brought freedom and truth for mankind through love. He laid down His life for us, thus uncovering the truth forevermore!

Today in the "war on the minds," through social media, movies, television, music, books, and influentials, the world spreads the lies so freely while church seems stuck in brick buildings. Change is upon us; GodAlmighty is raising up artists, writers, producers, actors, prophets, preachers, business people in every field to bring the truth to the world in creative ways that impact people wherever they are. True food for body, soul, and Spirit is in demand, and the end-time saints will be used to re-program the existing media platforms, movie theaters, radio stations, and chief pulpits. More importantly, outside these established venues in the grassroots society, the word is spreading, and the revolution has begun. The people will not take the status quo much longer. We must learn to wait on God, give Him everything and courageously surrender to Him; then He will form us into the creative vessels ready for this great end-time harvest. Only when we care not for ourselves will we be able to love every person around us. What are you doing with your life? What will it matter in eternity?

SACRED COWS

Now that you have been made free in Christ, let the truth continue to make you free, don't be confused and frustrated by traditional teaching or thought, have courage to revisit these subjects.

GOD ALLOWS OR GOD MEANT?

I hear Christians all the time saying,"God allowed this, God allowed that," but if He's God, is He really just sitting around allowing things to happen, or is He orchestrating things to fulfill a plan? We read chapter 50 in Genesis after Joseph was betrayed, cast off, and rose up to become the leader of all the world. When his brothers came back, weeping to ask for forgiveness, he said, "Don't worry, what you meant for evil—God meant for good." It was God's plan all along. The Hebrew word "meant" in Genesis 50:20 means "to fabricate." God didn't just "allow" Joseph to get captured, just like He didn't "allow" Jesus to be crucified. God planned it and orchestrated it to show us His love and glory. I find it very comforting to know that God has a plan, and He works daily in the affairs of man, whispering to the lost and the found, those that don't even acknowledge Him, and the faithful that do make everything work for their ultimate good.

ALL SIN THE SAME?

There's a cliche running through the body of Christ that all sin is the same. If you stole a piece of gum, you're just as guilty as a murderer. This is true in the context of salvation; we all need the blood of Christ to take away our sin, any sin, we all fell in Adam. But it sounds silly to people who don't know Christ because we all know sin is not all the same. Rape and murder are grave life-changing abominations, and the consequences thereof differ greatly from stealing a piece of gum and are on a whole different level. Because there are levels of sin, we have laws with the punishments appropriate to the crime as God has ordained in the Levitical law and reinforced in Romans chapter 13. Therefore, all sin is not the same.

DID GOD FORSAKE HIS SON?

My God, My God, why have You forsaken me? Most people think God has forsaken them. We hear all the time, "God can't look at sin," well, that would be bad news if you want to be a friend of God because who doesn't ever sin? The idea that God would not look at you because of sin is a silly lie, a traditional belief passed down by parrots repeating what other preachers say. Ironically, Psalm 22 proves God did not hide His face from Jesus and has not hidden His face from you; He is loving and faithful!

Look at Psalm 22. This beautiful messianic Psalm is often used to claim that God had to hide His face from His Son, Jesus, when He took the sin of the world upon Himself to save the elect. But, what really happened is that Jesus quoted the song's title on the cross to proclaim who he was and the faithfulness of God. "My God, my God, why do You forsake me?" was like the title of the song (psalm). See verse 24; this proves the opposite of what is traditionally taught:"-For He has not despised nor abhorred the affliction of the afflicted; nor has He hidden His face from Him; but when He cried to Him, He heard" (Psalm 22:24). David wrote this inspired messianic song from his life experience, and it also foretold the Messiah's moment to come.

The introduction of chapter and verse numbering came centuries later, so it was common to reference a particular passage by quoting a memorable line from it. Jesus quoted the first line of Psalm 22 to point His listeners towards it and help them understand He was fulfilling messianic prophecy.

Now read the whole psalm in context and know that Jesus is the Jewish Messiah, and God does not need to look away from His Son or you!

My God, My God, why have You forsaken Me?

Why are You so far from helping Me,

And from the words of My groaning?

O My God, I cry in the daytime, but You do not hear;

And in the night season, and am not silent.

But You are holy,

Enthroned in the praises of Israel.

Our fathers trusted in You;

They trusted, and You delivered them.

They cried to You and were delivered;

They trusted in You and were not ashamed.

But I am a worm and no man;

A reproach of men and despised by the people.

All those who see Me ridicule Me;

They shoot out the lip, they shake the head, saying,

"He trusted in the Lord, let Him rescue Him;

Let Him deliver Him since He delights in Him!"

But You are He who took Me out of the womb;

You made Me trust while on My mother's breasts.

I was cast upon You from birth.

From My mother's womb

You have been My God.

Be not far from Me,

For trouble is near;

For there is none to help.

Many bulls have surrounded Me;

Strong bulls of Bashan have encircled Me.

They gape at Me with their mouths,

Like a raging and roaring lion.

I am poured out like water,

And all My bones are out of joint;

My heart is like wax;

It has melted within Me.

113

WHY

My strength is dried up like a potsherd,

And My tongue clings to My jaws;

You have brought Me to the dust of death.

For dogs have surrounded Me;

The congregation of the wicked has enclosed Me.

They pierced My hands and My feet;

I can count all My bones.

They look and stare at Me.

They divide My garments among them,

And for My clothing they cast lots.

But You, O Lord, do not be far from Me;

O My Strength, hasten to help Me!

Deliver Me from the sword,

My precious life from the power of the dog.

Save Me from the lion's mouth

And from the horns of the wild oxen!

You have answered Me.

I will declare Your name to My brethren;

In the midst of the assembly, I will praise You.

You who fear the Lord, praise Him!

All you descendants of Jacob, glorify Him,

And fear Him, all you offspring of Israel!

For He has not despised nor abhorred the affliction of the afflicted;

Nor has He hidden His face from Him;

But when He cried to Him, He heard.

My praise shall be of You in the great assembly;

I will pay My vows before those who fear Him.

The poor shall eat and be satisfied;

Those who seek Him will praise the Lord.

Let your heart live forever!

WHY

All the ends of the world

Shall remember and turn to the Lord,

And all the families of the nations

Shall worship before You.

For the kingdom is the Lord's,

And He rules over the nations.

All the prosperous of the earth

Shall eat and worship;

All those who go down to the dust

Shall bow before Him,

Even he who cannot keep himself alive.

A posterity shall serve Him.

It will be recounted of the Lord to the next generation,

They will come and declare His righteousness to a people who will be born,

That He has done this.

BAPTISM NAMES?

Much controversy has been discussed about how to baptize and in what name, but let's cut to the chase. After the resurrection of our Savior,in Acts 2:38, it says: "Then Peter said to them, 'Repent,[change your mind] and let every one of you be baptized in the name of Jesus Christ for the remission of sins; and you shall receive the gift of the Holy Spirit'" (brackets added for clarity). All through the book of Acts, the baptism of the apostles was done in the name of Jesus Christ, not in "the Father, the Son, and the Holy Spirit," as all religious denominations do today. The reason Jesus stated in Matthew 28 go forth and baptize in the "name" (singular not plural) of the Father, the Son, the Holy Spirit is that Jesus Christ is the name of the Father, the Son, and the Holy Spirit.

> For unto us a child is born, unto us a child is given: and the government shall be upon his shoulder: and his name shall be called Wonderful, Counselor, The mighty God, The everlasting Father, The Prince of Peace.

Isaiah 9:6 (KJV)

Isaiah shows us that Jesus is the everlasting Father; He's also the Word of God and the Son. He and the Holy Spirit and the Father are one. Considering this and the apostles' example in Acts, why would we want to be baptized in any other name? If you have already been baptized in the Father, the Son,and the Holy Spirit, that's okay, but hopefully, we can see the revelation of Christ, follow the example of the apostles, and baptize in the name above every name henceforth, the name Jesus Christ.

ATONEMENT, EXPIATION OR PROPITIATION?

Paul writes in Hebrews that we are now part of a new and better covenant, actually a testament, and part of that testament is our sins were completely taken away by the Lamb of God. God in the flesh, fulfilling all prophecy of physical animals which were sacrificed in the old covenant, the lesser covenant which only temporarily atoned for (covered sin) until the final sacrifice of God's Son, the Lamb we worship, expiated our sin. True liberty comes from knowing that our sins are taken away and forgotten by the Almighty, by the gift of His Son's blood, not just covered and still lingering against us.

"For it is not possible for the blood of bulls and goats could take away sins" (Hebrews 10:4).

IS THERE AN OLD TESTAMENT?

Today people call the older books of the Bible the Old Testament, but in reality, there is actually no such thing as an "old testament." There is an old covenant written in Deuteronomy 28 when God gives conditional promises to Israel, such as if you keep these rules, you will be blessed, and if you don't, you will be cursed. The New Testament is completely different from a will, in which we, as sons, receive an inheritance just because we are sons, not based on conditions. This is made possible only because of the death of a testator, Jesus Christ. We are now part of a new and better covenant that is a testament.

And for this reason, He is the Mediator of the new covenant, by means of death, for the redemption of the transgressions under the first covenant, that those who are called may receive the promise of the eternal inheritance. The Mediator's death is necessary for where there is a testament; there must also of necessity be the death of the testator. For a testament is in force after men are dead since it has no power at all while the testator lives (Hebrews 9:15-17).

ANTI-CHURCH

Is there anything "real" in the world anymore? We live in the "end of the age," and we see clearly now the "revelation" of all things. Evil is manifest on talk shows where "vampires" tell of eating flesh and lesbian sex. Righteousness is seen in true Christians serving and loving the unlovable, not to mention Bible prophecies fulfilled every day. But, the real cry in the hearts of many is, "Give me something real!" There is a woman at the grocery check-out with her artificially sweetened diet-cola, wearing man-made synthetic fabric to cover her man-made silicon breasts,and she is late to a "New Age" Unity church meeting where she will learn of an "imitation" Jesus.

The truth is the only way we become free, and the real Jesus is the only one who can set us free. The world has seen the Pope and false teachers, but these fake people have only caused the name of God to be blasphemed. God's agenda has always been to be properly represented here on the earth. God is "real," He is genuine. That is why He came in the flesh to show us what He is like. Now, He takes us through death, burial and resurrection, the trials, the waiting, and the whole process to make us genuine Christians, not fake people running around quoting His word out of context. Jesus was not too "professional" to talk to the "woman at the well,"

He wasn't too busy to relate to the "little people." When we know that God is God, we are free to be loving, patient, and kind, people with no greater agenda than to serve and love others. Most Christians are consumed and driven to "get ahead," have the "American dream," which they have been trained to call "prosperity." Many pastors are consumed and driven to build the biggest church, increase the number of souls, the level of tithes, whatever, to make something happen so they will be significant. All these works of the flesh can be summed up in: "All that is in the world is the lust of the eyes, the lust of the flesh and the boastful pride of life." The Word goes on to say that those who love these things have not "the love of the Father" (1 John 2:15-17).

While we all wait for the real Jesus to return, we are bombarded by imitations; it is the "age of imitation." You have heard of the Ice Age, the Bronze Age, even the information age; well, this is the age of imitation. Before Jesus does come, we will see a fake Jesus come, the Antichrist (2 Thessalonians chapter 2). Jesus warned in Matthew 24 that many would say, "I am Christ." What he refers to here is not only that many will come and say they are a Messiah, but also many will come and say they are "anointed." The Anointed One, the Christ, only works in the truth, and the truth is real! People who walk in truth are free to be real, with no facades. With no agenda but to please God, we are free from the pretense that causes us to build up walls by putting on airs or projecting an image.

God is not represented properly by leaders in churches who have not cooperated with His death, burial, and resurrection (sanctification). This problem produces what I call "the anti-church." Anti is a Greek word meaning "instead of" substitute, or fake. In other words, the anti-church has an agenda and does many things instead of God's plan for the church. Only people who have been through the process of death, burial, and resurrection can see and manifest the kingdom of God and not steal His glory. The Antichrist is not the devil; it is man trying to be God (Revelation 13:18). When man submits to God, waits on God, and does nothing until God moves, then and only then is a true work of the Spirit manifest.Satan has tricked people into playing God since the Garden of Eden; has he tricked you?

As I turned the radio through the various stations, I noticed the rock and rollers were high energy, abandoned in passion; in fact, all "secular" stations are vibrant and full of life, but the "Christian" radio station has a woman saying, "I'm depressed, I am lonely, I need prayer." Now, wait a minute, these are people with God, right? Then the realization hit me; the church or, I should say, "anti-church" just kills people; they are drained of all freedom and life and become slaves of the religious system. Instead of floating through God's beautiful creation, full of joy from salvation and love from Jesus, many Christians are bored, tired, and confused, or they have already given up on "church," and they are "hiding" in the world. In the days when Jesus walked the earth, the religious system was run by power-hungry Pharisees, controlling people to build their big "ministries," Jesus taught all the discouraged people out on the side of a mountain. He set them free with truth. He didn't use them to build a big ministry. When David was in the cave with all the misfits, and Saul was running Israel in the flesh, the remnant was underground; it is the same today. The wheat and the tares grow up together; some church leaders operate in the spirit, some in the flesh. No one can take Jesus from you, no one can take your true friends, but our problem is: the larger the group, the more temptation for the flesh. God wants his people to grow up, know the word, know Him personally, grounded in love, and then we won't be tossed to and fro by the doctrines of these "super Christians" at giant crusades wearing silk suits,where big offerings are the rule.

The present condition of the "official" church can be summed up in two major extremes:

1) The mainline, watered down, boring, denominational "old guard" church. These are seminary-fed and conservative and don't really apply to our "real life." We enter the big building each Sunday morning, joined by the big bells and a steeple,we sense of feeling of awe, and we are humbled by this great institution, but after an hour or so, we're looking at our watch because the

guy in the robe is so boring. The church I read about in the Bible in the book of Acts is so much more exciting and real.

2) The second extreme is the sensational and emotionally fulfilling "charismatic" church. With contemporary rock and roll music and a "really big show," there is never a dull moment as we are told endless promises of God's love and available power for us to be healthy, wealthy, and wise. We are invited to "shake our booty" for the Lord, give all our money, so God will make us rich, then imagine and confess our dream life, and God has to give it to us. The fact is God gave gifts to the church to love the world and equip the church, but the "faith" teachers have taught the charismatic how to use the word for personal gain, which is witchcraft (1Corinthians 12-14).

The true church is called to preach the gospel to every creature and equip the saints for the work of the ministry. The Word of Faith preachers have made it by merchanding the flock (2 Peter 2:1-3). The "faith" message was that popularized in the '80s; it was a move of God to get people out of a defeated, poverty mentality. Since then, many have taken this message out of balance, and it is now perverted. Any agenda that is held higher than "Christ being formed and you" is a wrong agenda. God's agenda is the only true and eternal agenda. All Christians know this down deep.

Why can't we major on Love instead of Love being an afterthought comment the quiet lady says after hours of discussion on every other subject? The true church is pictured *in the book of Acts* where people were excited about Jesus, meeting every night in their homes in fellowship and prayer, excited about Jesus Himself, not out selling a church or a ministry. The church is again coming to this reality as more and more Christians know Jesus through the shaking. Otherwise, we are no different than the cults like Mormons or Jehovah's Witnesses.

Throughout the history of God dealing with man, the relationship has been based on sacrifice, from the first animal slain to cover Adam and Eve to the Son of God, given to us as the lamb on the cross. The modern-day American gospel has no sacrifice. Jesus is portrayed as a big genie giving temporal gifts to brat children in these "Success in Life" circles. We have been called to live in the eternal perspective to serve the Living God, not use God to have the best of Disney culture while forgetting the call to feed the sheep and reach the world. Leaders of the Body of Christ are called to a life of sacrifice (Romans 12:1-2), not success in worldly values. Today many Christians see these covetous men who fleece the flock as examples of people who are blessed by God when in reality, they are using God's people for personal gain. Men who use the Word and gifts to build their own kingdoms and cause people to look to them instead of God are cutting people off from a personal relationship with God just like the Pope; this is"Antichrist." We have seen so many wrong examples, caricatures of Christians. Now is the time to look at Jesus. He is a perfect example of how to spend your life to God's glory. Everything He did is relevant to our life, except we do not need to die on the cross. It is finished.

The "faith perverts" tell us that we do the miracles by controlling the elements through the "force of faith."The same old message the serpent used in the Garden of Eden, "You can be God."This charismatic witchcraft is a subtle deception because we do have power as sons of God in Jesus' name. The test we must apply to our actions is whether we are obedient to the Lord or using our power in His Word to get what we want or what He wants. Love seeks not its own way (1Corinthians 13:5).

WHAT IS GOD DOING? WHAT IS MAN DOING?

-"What is God doing?"—"Networking people together in mutually beneficial and eternal relationships."

"What is Man doing?"—"Using God's Word to build institutions to control people for personal gain" (Nicolaitans—[nico-conquer, laitans—people], Revelation 2:1).

-The true church (real) Jesus—Jesus says, "I will build My church and the gates of Hell shall not prevail against it."

The anti-church (instead of) man—pastor says, "We must build this church at any cost!" The Bible says, "We are commanded to make disciples; God does the rest."

-"Be My Spirit"—by divine appointment, the Holy Spirit network joins the body together in mutually beneficial relationships. People set free by real love and anointed ministry spread the Word and bring friends to receive love.

By Tradition—through promotional means, programs, advertising, and trying what has been successful for other churches. Efforts are directed to bring crowds for big offerings to keep the big façade going "feed the machine."

-People—we are the temple of God. First Peter 2:5 shows us that God only sees the people he has redeemed as "His House."

Buildings—we must live to keep the building up and growing. Members' resources are depleted to save the "Mother Church." Time, money, and energy devoted to building program and maintenance could be more fruitful by going to people with the gospel and gifts.

-All glory to Jesus—there is one special guy, and it is not you or me. In Corinthians 6:4, we see God's heart about who is special and who is not. How many pastors ask the quiet little lady in the back of the church to help solve a problem or reach souls?

Glorify man—church growth experts or whoever's works are held in higher esteem than the Holy Bible, the Word of God! God is angry about this.

-The Cross—when the financial burden is gone, we are free to preach the whole word of God, all the "hard sayings," all the controversial issues, the death to self which really sets people free, the truth!

Compromise—when church growth and financial responsibility are the concern, pastors must not be too controversial and must not offend anyone with their true convictions because some mayleave the church (peace = growth).

-Control—the true church is led by no one but the Holy Spirit and may seem out of control to the flesh.

Controlled—the anti-church is controlled by IRS 501 3-C regulations; the government's definition of a cult is not the same as the bible states. Leaders who feel threatened by the flock also hinder the flow of the Holy Spirit; by not allowing every member to speak at meetings, we miss out on the revelations God has put in each heart.

-All members minister—"How is it then, brethren? when ye come together, everyone of you hath a psalm, hath a doctrine, hath a tongue, hath a revelation, hath an interpretation. Let all things be done unto edifying" (1 Corinthians 14:26, KJV).

Clergy-Layman Lie—the "special" ones are on the platform.

Truth—people's true gifts and callings are manifest in real-life situations, not because of titles or positions.

-Leaders—dead to self, let go of all ambition and vainglory, and know that the church is God's responsibility; our only job is to speak the truth in love. God builds His church; true shepherds only want to serve and bless the flock.

Anti-leaders—ambition, search for significance drives men to build big churches to prove to God they love Him or

131

prove their family they really are a minister, etc. (flesh).

-Apostolic (sent out)—the true church is joined to facilitate and equip each member in His calling and destiny. To "send out" God's people, in the dream, He has put their heart to bring His kingdom come (Ephesians 4:1-6). The church today is attracting crowds with promises of healing, prosperity, happiness, and fun but is not equipped to stand in the evil day to come.

Anti-apostolic (keep in)—the anti-church uses people to meet its needs, like a bottomless pit, the members' money is all sucked into the big machine, the members' gifts lie dormant while they are "reformed" to fit the positions the church must fill to keep in business. While most members, week after week, just standup, sitdown, and say amen, the real zealous ones get excited about God and want to do something for Him, so they volunteer for everything, and they end up burned out. The anti-church imports big names to keep and "grow" the flock, but worse, it keeps people in the pews rather than sending them out to build the kingdom.

As the antichrist or self-righteous Spirit is "Joshua-ed" out of our hearts, we become true worshipers. As the anti-church or traditional mentality and program are rooted out of church, we will become the true "house of glory" that God desires to see every time we meet. The Pharisees were self-righteous, and they were the promoters of tradition. Jesus told them, "Your traditions make the word of God of no effect!" This is serious; we must repent (change our mind) about how we "have church." It is scary to pioneer new ground, but what do we have to lose? When we die to self and have to depend on Jesus, then we grow and the treasure that He has put in us comes out. The gifts and love in the body of Christ cannot grow when Saul's armor is weighing down the anointing, the liberty in the very life of God. The "professional" attitude at churches does not allow true friendships to grow,and the result is an intimidating atmosphere. True "friends" can flow together; say anything to each other and liberty is the banner where there is no pretense. The true church is people and can be found in every country, city, and street all over the world. In every business, church, and school, God has elected a remnant, but in Revelation 18:4, he says come out of the wicked system, and that is a test of whether we love our life or not.

APOSTOLIC MANIFESTATION

What does God mean when He says, "Come out of the Whore of Babylon, my people?" (Revelation 18:4) Is He talking about the catholic church in Rome or New York City, the seat of trade, and the United Nations? Babylon is a system that transcends economic, political, and religious structures. In the Spirit realm, the powers of darkness have wanted to control man and traffic souls (Revelation 18:13) since Lucifer fell and became Satan, the head of Babylon or the world system. "Love not the world" is the command to the ecclesia, the church, the called-out ones; we are called out of the world into the eternal kingdom(1 John 2:15-17). This is a large can of worms, but for now, let us touch on the history of the church.

Beginning with the apostolic outreach of the original apostles, the church was persecuted and spread throughout the world. The church was so foreign to society, then Satan"legalized"Christianity under Rome in AD325 and blended all religions together; everyone was a "Christian." Truth took the backseat to profitability and compromise. The point here, however, is that since the Reformation, when God sovereignly shook the world through the revelation "the just shall live by faith," we have seen nothing but more than the roman catholic false priesthood remodeled and remodeled over and over again. Denominations have been formed since the Reformation, building on one revelation after another, for example, Martin Luther—Lutherans, Wesley—Methodist, Baptist, etc.Once a denomination is formed, it never goes away. Today, denominations are like chain restaurants with corporate headquarters, centralized government controlling the message, methods, and finances. Yes, great revivals were birthed from many movements since the Reformation, bringing us to where we are today, but the mindset of leadership was always attached to the clergy-layman perspective engraved on men's souls by satan's model in Rome. We must see Jesus' original plan for a lasting revival and a new reformation of church government. The apostle will find his place in leadership, and finally, the church will be taught how to live in unity to affect our civilization, to turn the world upside-down. The body of Christ spends 10 percentof its finances at the "church" and 90 percent in the world. The end-time apostolic church will rule in the marketplace using God's principles. Many corporations are smart enough to meet Christian's needs with Christian stores, but how much of their profits go back to the kingdom of God? The wealth of the wicked is laid up for the righteous, yes, but only when the leadership of the Body of Christ releases the flock to do great exploits, instead of sitting in the pew and supporting merchandisers on TV with their time and money, will we see God's plan manifest. The end-time apostolic church will look more like Abraham or Joseph, owning businesses to teach the world God's ways, and less like the Levites, living in the church building and pointing fingers at the world which produces movies, theme parks, and controls public opinion. God wants the Body of Christ free and equipped to manifest God's kingdom in the religious, economic, and political realms. Like Solomon, we will confound the world with the wisdom of God, and the kings of the world will come and see how we live and be left breathless like the queen of Sheeba. Today we are at the threshold of the End time apostolic manifestation. Only the anointing of the Holy Spirit can break the yoke of bondage to the world system, allowing us to set trends with the Creator in our heart, no longer copying the world in music, methods, and culture. The two kingdoms are dividing more and more, the kingdom of God and the kingdom of Satan. People wonder why so-called Christians go to church but live like the world. Knowing little of the Word of God or God's ways, most believers think that the church denominations are relatively biblical, some more in line with God's blueprint than others. Let me tell you, today, all denominations areobsolete. The Roman Catholic pyramid is upside down, and every church with one man in control is only a remodel of the false church. Some of the true church is inside the whore, the wheat and the tares grow up together, but today is the day of no more compromise, God is moving His bulldozer through the earth as apostles and prophets to "pluck up, tear down and replant" (Jeremiah

1:10) the people of God in true love and relationships, and under-shepherds that serve Him, not their own desires. All over the country, Christian leaders are saying, "Revival is coming; we are praying for revival." Yes, revival is coming and has been, but it doesn't remain because of our structures and mindsets. Right now, all over the country, God is purging and shaking the mindsets and motives in the church. There is a grassroots revolution going on; pastors are saying, "I don't care if I have a church; I want God!" Members are challenging leadership and the status quo with the simplicity of the gospel and servanthood. A new form of government is arising as the apostolic church emerges in our midst, like a butterfly coming forth from the cocoon of what the church has been doing. People will no longer travel across the world to "revival" or some big name "revivalist" to get a hold of God; God is everywhere and about to pour out His glory on the true Body of Christ. Those who let go of position and power, things of the flesh and tradition, will move to the next level of power and the truth, while those who hold onto the pews and "their ministry" will be swept away in the flood of God's Spirit. We were pilgrims here and own nothing; the end-time Bride will be free and operate above and beyond all present traditions and financial constraints. God will no longer tolerate the tax on her any more than His Word and anointing. The common "layman" on the back row with the Word of the Lord will be heard, even by the big-name super-stars, or God will send judgment to prove His Word and His servant, no matter how insignificant he may seem. Judgment begins first in the house of God and has begun. Sovereignly, God wanted the whole world to manifest as it has to this point, don't think for a minute God is worried about men controlling His people. Just as David was abused by Saul into becoming the king God wanted, so we have begun going through the fire of oppression for such a time as this. Just like the blind man, then Jesus healed, and all asked, "Why was this man blind? Was it his parents' sin or his?" Jesus said, "Neither, but for the glory of God, for the display of God's power." So it is today when the heart cries across the Body of Christ is "give me more, give me liberty or give me death!" We are about to see "nobodies" rise up in the power of the truth and the bricks are "gonna" shake. The polarity caused by this outpouring of the Holy Spirit will cause the apostasy, the falling away of many church people, many will compromise to hold onto buildings, power, position, and the mall, but on the side of truth and love, God will supernaturally convene to bring David and his soldiers from the cave and into kingship with apostolic authority like fire, burning up all religion, control and "church abuse." Yes, we will be persecuted by the religious and the world, what's new. Only jealousy for the glory of God will initiate and sustain you in this battle. God's love is eternal; who else can guarantee reward? (Philippians 1:27-2:1-4) The apostle does not want to build on another man's foundation. The end-time harvest that everyone is talking about is coming, but not until the apostolic network is set up. The harvest of new converts is not going to be sent to the existing traditional Saul like structure; God is purging all churches to get them founded on the apostolic principles, if they do not conform to His image of change, they will be left out of the coming harvest, which will be a result of the shaking of Babylon. Babylon is comfortable, we all like it to some extent, but God is faithful to shake things and stretch us beyond what we think we can do to fulfill vision and destiny.

The house of God has been under remodeling since the Reformation, the prophets, like painters, trying to make everyone "see it right." The Evangelists have operated like electricians, working to charge us with power, no matter the floor plan. The pastors have been plumbing the best they know how to supply water to the flock and rid us of waste and problems. The Teachers have worked on this detail or that, but today the apostles are stepping up to set things in order. A new house of God is being built; only the apostle confirms the house; he reads God's blueprint and sets the other four offices in order like a general contractor.Now the five-fold ministry will manifest with all members operating freely in their gift, not hindered by or limited by the old house. The new house has a new government for the end-time Bride, and all will benefit from the liberty that is produced.

The tension that is present in this process of transition from church as we know it and the apostolic reality we all long for is a result of people with God-ordained vision working with and under others who have a vision of their own. We must be careful not to label people as independent or unteachable because they do not march the way we say march. God has made each of us march his drum, not man's drum. Jesus is the head, and we are the body. When we let go of our ideas of how it should be and refuse to form people into our image, then we will witness people bloom into the flower God has made them be, reproducing after their kind, apostolic works to build the kingdom, not our kingdoms. The days of ministry heads using the flock to build great churches to their glory are over. Each person is a plant, to sew seed and produce fruit for the master. If we men try to prune the plant in any other way than the unique design God has for that person will diminish the creative process of God's making a vessel of honor. Therefore, the tension we experience is necessary for change; as Calebs and Joshuas rise up with new ways and unorthodox perspectives, this challenges existing leadership, and the wise, we will know that these challenges are in no way dishonoring or unappreciative of elders. The problem is, we have not been here before; the answer is, Jesus, the apostle of our faith, has a plan.

We have now discussed abuse of power through church government versus God's design. The simple truth is that Jesus is *the Good Shepherd*, men may borrow money, build a building and write "*church*" on it, but it is God who puts people in our life to learn from. We must be faithful with divine appointments to feed the sheep because on these matters will we be judged.

People under a "pastor's" vision to support and bring to pass his interpretation of God's plan depend on "pastor" instead of the Holy Spirit.

Hopefully, we all stand on Jesus Christ with elders and leaders supporting the body. The big vision is to build up and facilitate all members in the vision God has given them to serve Christ. We all see in part; we all prophecy in part (1 Corinthians 13). Instead of Israel looking to Saul or waiting on David, the whole army is joining in the fight.

It has become obvious that even in America, government control will force the church underground as she has operated all over the world since the book of Acts. Apostles, prophets, and pastors will lead and serve in house churches as the Body of Christ is refined in the midst of persecution. America has enjoyed freedom like no other country, but presently freedom is under attack with pandemic lockdowns and civil unrest; therefore, the day of the underground church is here.

MANIFESTATION OF FIVE-FOLD MINISTRY REALITY

The church began as an apostolic work, and the church age will end as a Bride of Christ is translated into glory after the final apostolic manifestation prepares her for the returning husbandman.In recent history, we have seen the restoring of the five-fold ministries. First, the "healing evangelists" of the '50s and '60s, the teaching movement of the '70s, which also raised up pastoral role identity, and then the restoring of the prophets through the 1980s, which continues now; these all happened during seasons with particular emphasis. Not until the apostolic mantle is fully realized will we experience the other four gifts to the body, all working simultaneously and in integrated harmony. Church meetings will really be spontaneous (Corinthians 14:26). The apostolic oversight is the support for all of our arms of ministry. Until now, leaders have always exhorted and encourage the body to wake up and live for God; like "mule," the body of Christ has been "kicked" by the pastors, prophets, evangelists, and teachers. Oh, praise to be God, for now, we are entering a season when the latter rain outpouring, coupled with the ripening of the vineyard, will cause us to see and apostolic leadership with their hands full, just trying to "bridal" the body of Christ as a

143

"stallion" full of faith. With the explosion of the discouraged returning, the harvest of new souls, churches will be over-crowded, and faithful ones who have been "on the shelf" will be launched into pastoral positions calling on elders for wisdom and guidance. These apostles have been learning the hard way for years and will be perfectly fit for the needs of these Phillips and Stephens. When the five-fold ministry is a reality, the Lord will add to the church daily as we have never seen in modern times, like in Acts 2:47.

We are experiencing an outpouring of the Holy Spirit, and God has revealed to many of his prophets an order for the church to become unified. First church renewal, second backsliders restored, then third the harvest of new converts. To accomplish this great change successfully, leadership now in "control" must identify giftings and callings and train their flock to become the household of faith that will contain the harvest. (A net with no holes) Where no vision is the people perish, many people are seeing the end-time vision of the victorious Bride, yet many of these least esteemed members of the body have no voice, many leaders are playing games spending time impressing each other; meanwhile, the Holy Spirit is given true worshipers revelation of this functional body. Most backsliders are discouraged because of two major problems.

1. Lack of revelation of God's grace and foundational truth in the sovereign work of salvation. The reality

of His unconditional love.

2. Their gifts and callings have not been nurtured; they feel they have no purpose, that the Christian life is sitting in a chair paying tithes. Our responsibility as shepherds is to discern the Body of Christ, to know what the flock needs, identify their gifts and purpose, discern timing for training or loose them into the works God has for them (Ephesians2:10). Accountability is pictured in Paul's letter to Timothy to encourage him and his calling to the glory of God. Paul is bringing Timothy into account of what God the Father had entrusted him to accomplish; this type of encouragement is rare.

The bottom line is that the gifts to the body of Christ are people, vessels of God's love, and we all need more love. When leadership stifles gifted members of the body, we all suffer. The glory of God is covering the whole earth. Get in the river!

WARFARE

When we have God's vision, not man's vision, the mind of Christ, nothing can stop us; we are in unity. It is time for all men to repent, change their mindset about the kingdom of God, not just the lost, even you must rethink your lifestyle, your motives. Jesus said, "Satan has come and found nothing in me," His mission was apostolic, to die for us. He emptied himself to the lowest place to be the foundation of the house. Our lifestyle and mindset are our warfare. In 2 Corinthians 10, Paul writes defending his authority as an apostle reminding the church we fight with the Word of truth. Then to Timothy he writes; No one engaged in warfare entangles himself in the affairs of this life, that he may please him who enlisted him as a soldier. 2 Timothy 2.4 The "weapons of our warfare" are spiritual truth and literally means "to be busy about an apostolic career of hardship and danger." From the Greek word "hoplon" and "strateia," we see the proper perspective of this chapter, "hoplon" means tool, shield, but to the Greek, it meant the "act of," nothing specific as physical sword or shovel, but the act."Strateia" comes from the root "host", which means encamp, or base camp, even host of angels. The literal meaning Paul is trying to get across here is "to serve in a military campaign, to execute the apostolic with its arduous duty and function, to contend with carnal inclinations." When we have the perspective that we are in a war, stationed on this planet, dead to the lust of the world, and receiving orders and authority from the base camp in heaven, 99 percent of our warfare is done. Christians struggle every day trying to have the "American dream" and serve a God for an eternal purpose. Like driving their cars with the gas on and the brakes on at the same time, burn—out and confusion results, not to mention a powerless life. Many believe that Chapter 10 is teaching people to scream at and divide the demons, but the demons just laugh; they know the secret of the war, it is loyalty to the commander. Unity in the spirit and faithfulness to the call will allow us to say, "Satan has come and found nothing in me." In fact, God uses the demons to show us the carnal nature that still has a place in our lives. You can bind the spirit of lust all you want, but if you are still lusting, it isn't bound. When we have the heart to serve like Christ, then we walk in love; we have no ambition, vainglory, or covetousness. The church is tormented by demons because the members covet worldly goods or even climb the corporate ladder in the church. The leadership is demonized when they try to control God's people, to have a big church, or live off the sheep's income. Jesus is the apostle of our faith; He neither lived off the sheep nor tried to be in power. When the people were trying to make Him a worldly king, He disappeared. Paul learned apostolic warfare from the Spirit of Christ. We must see ourselves as pilgrims here, servants of God and every human being on the planet, and then we will demonstrate the love of Christ to the world,and the kingdom of God is manifest. We just do our little part, and God does the rest. The exhortation from Paul to Timothy (2 Timothy 2:4) is clear, saints of the highest God, ambassadors of Christ, are soldiers here on earth. Our calling is eternal, and we're not to be entangled in the affairs of this life. Why is warfare not a matter of formulas and chasing demons? Our success as soldiers of Christ all depends on motives of the heart and walking in love, preferring our brothers and sisters above ourselves. God is love; brethren, keep yourself from idols.

THE COURSE
OF THE WORD

These are the steps of the Christian Life

The Word Becoming Flesh, first in Messiah—then in us

Receive Word Luke 1:26-38

Christ Born in Mary, so Christ can be born in you.

Proclamation Luke 1:46-56 2:27-32 (Prophecy) Something new is in me, and it must come out!

Misunderstanding Luke 2:42-50 (By Family, Friends)

Baptism Luke 3:21-22 (It's not our idea)

Wilderness Luke 4:1-13 Temptation (overcome by the Word)

Confrontation with flesh Luke 4:16-22, 28-30

Ministry Miracles (Popularity) John 6:2 & 26, John 2:23-25

Matthew 9:8, Matthew 8:19

Expose Flesh Unpopular (Pharisees) (666) John 6:66

Matthew 12:14 Persecuted by Flesh Galatians 4:29

Betrayal (Rejection) Luke 22:21&48, John 18:27,

Luke 23:18-23

Gethsemane Luke 22:42-44 "NOT MINE BUT THINE"

Trial (Falsely Accused) Isaiah 53:7, Luke 23:2-15,

Matthew 26:57-68

Wrongful Death Luke 23:46, Isaiah 53:6,9

Burial Matthew 27:58-60

Resurrection Matthew 28:5-6

Unbelief by Followers Luke 24:37-39, Matthew 28:17

Overcome World Luke 23:34

Rule & Reign Through Others Matthew 28:18

OUR FAITH IS TESTED AT EVERY STEP,

HOPE IS FORMED, AND LOVE MOTIVATES US

TO YIELD TO THE HOLY SPIRIT.

EARTHLY-SPIRITUALTYPES

OLD ADAM-NEW ADAM

of the earth (ADAM) from above (JESUS)

CARNAL MAN-NEW MAN (2Corinthians5:17)

Jacob, Israel

Goliath (Flesh) David (Vessel)

Abram,Abraham

Saul,Paul

CARNAL MIND-NEW MIND

Golgotha/Skull Hill, Mind of Christ

(Matthew 27:33) (Romans 8:7) (1 Corinthians 1:16)

MOSES-JESUS

(Temporary Deliverer) (Eternal Deliverer)

WHY

OLD COVENANT-NEW COVENANT

(Testament)

Mt. Sinai, Mount Zion

(Law) (Grace)

(Flesh) (Spirit)

Hagar—Ishmael, Jerusalem—Isaac

(Galatians 4:22-31)

OLD STONES-NEW STONES

(Buildings) (People)

(Nehemiah 4:2) (1 Peter 2:5)

OLD CITY-NEW CITY

Jerusalem-New Jerusalem

(Revelation 21:2)

(Physical) (Spiritual)

OLD KING-NEW KING

David,Jesus (Revelation 19:16)

(Sinned) (Perfect)

ABOUT THE AUTHOR

Russell David Hobbs was born in Lubbock, Texas, in 1958 and grew up in Dallas, Texas. His exodus from suburbia led him to pioneer the art movement in historic Deep Ellum, which had become a ghost town east of downtown Dallas in the early 1980s until 1987. That is when his janitor preached Christ to him, and he was radically saved. Russell poured out all the liquor, canceled fiftybands, and became a witness of the resurrection.

Like Nebuchadnezzar, his conversion greatly affected the kingdom he had built, and he immediately networked to evangelize and serve the lost artists, runaways, and street people, and influentials of Dallas with the gospel. The Holy Spirit led him to the wilderness of East Texas from 1991 to 1994to be "buried," and he has been "resurrected" to proclaim the kingdom of God, teaching, training, and equipping the saints of God in a local body in the apostolic movement to perfect the Body of Christ.

CPSIA information can be obtained
at www.ICGtesting.com
Printed in the USA
LVHW011148290721
693955LV00013B/377

9 781637 693360